A Twist *of* Lemmon

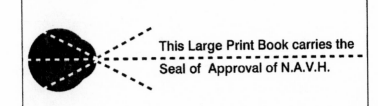

This Large Print Book carries the
Seal of Approval of N.A.V.H.

A Twist *of* Lemmon

A TRIBUTE TO MY FATHER

Chris Lemmon

Thorndike Press • Waterville, Maine

Copyright © 2006 by Chris Lemmon.

Published in 2006 by arrangement with Algonquin Books of Chapel Hill, a division of Workman Publishing Co., Inc.

Thorndike Press® Large Print Biography.

The tree indicium is a trademark of Thorndike Press.

The text of this Large Print edition is unabridged.
Other aspects of the book may vary from the original edition.

Set in 16 pt. Plantin.

Printed in the United States on permanent paper.

Library of Congress Cataloging-in-Publication Data

Lemmon, Chris, 1954–
    A twist of Lemmon : a tribute to my father / by Chris Lemmon.
        p. cm. — (Thorndike Press large print biography.)
    ISBN 0-7862-8814-0 (lg. print : hc : alk. paper)
    1. Lemmon, Jack.   2. Motion picture actors and actresses — United States — Biography.   3. Large type books.
I. Title.   II. Series: Thorndike Press large print biography series.
PN2287.L42L46 2006b
791.4302′8092—dc22
    [B]   2006013555

To Pop — I'll never forget.

FOREWORD

I first met Mr. Lemmon when I was thirteen years of age. My drama class from junior high school took a trip to the Mark Taper Forum in Los Angeles to see a performance of *Juno and the Paycock* starring Walter Matthau, Maureen Stapleton, and Jack Lemmon. I remember vividly the workshop we all attended with the cast prior to the play, and the generous words of encouragement that all three actors gave to our group. When the session ended, I walked up to Mr. Lemmon and asked him to sign an 8" × 10" picture of him that I had brought with me. While he was giving me his autograph, I asked him what advice he had for a young actor. He looked me directly in the eye and said that if I was serious about wanting a career, I should consider going to New York to study theater.

Six years later I took his advice and attended the Juilliard School of Drama in Manhattan. A few years after that I auditioned to play Mr. Lemmon's alcoholic son in the classic Eugene O'Neill play *Long*

Day's Journey into Night. That audition was a major turning point in my career, but even more important was the effect it had on my life.

For the audition, I prepared several scenes from the play, and Mr. Lemmon was there to perform with the actors trying out. I got to play about four scenes with him, and it was a truly remarkable experience. I recall I was somewhat relentless with my attack on the role and really gave it to Mr. Lemmon with both barrels blazing. At the end of the reading, he walked up to me, put his hand on my shoulder, and said, "I never thought I'd find the rotten kid, but you're it. Jesus Christ, what the hell was that?"

I won the role, and opened a chapter in my life, headed in a direction that I've endeavored to follow throughout my career. My guide was, and remains, Mr. Lemmon. He became my mentor, and while I eventually did start calling him Jack, somehow referring to him as Mr. Lemmon in this foreword allows me to offer him the nod of deep respect that I believe he deserves.

Observing him day after day in that year-long production — through rehearsals, dinners, lunches, events, late nights, early mornings, flights, car trips, piano playing, golfing, dog walking, and everything in between — as we moved from Durham, North Carolina, to Washington, D.C., to New York, to London, to Israel, and finally to Toronto, was the greatest lesson of professional humility that a young actor could hope to receive. My memories of Mr. Lemmon are vibrant and indelible, and his wisdom and words of guidance continue to inspire me to this day. He was a man who anyone could be enormously proud to know, and most especially anyone who has ever called himself an actor. He was a credit to his profession because he was a person whose humanity was bigger than his talent. And when you think for a moment about the size and depth of that talent, then you begin to understand how seriously he took his role as a human being. He was generous, committed, loyal, trusting, compassionate, and one of the funniest people you would ever be likely to meet. But he not only enjoyed making others laugh, he loved to laugh himself, and did so continuously throughout the years I worked with him (in three other films).

If you ask me what I learned in his presence, the answers come tumbling out. Most important, I learned about behavior, for he exemplified the way you should treat the people around you — always making sure your coworkers feel important and confident, and are having an enjoyable experience. I realized that being an actor — in Mr. Lemmon's case, not just an actor, but also a major film star — elevates you into a position of responsibility because everyone around you looks to you as a leader. Playing a major character in a film or stage production puts an actor at the center of the experience, and the likeability and relatability of the actor can have an enormous effect in creating a pleasurable atmosphere for everyone involved, most especially the audience. I've seen actors playing major parts who do not achieve this level of likeability, and the work suffers. I've seen some examples of bad behavior by stars that would light your hair on fire. Mr. Lemmon would only light your heart, and, of course, tap your funny bone.

He always knew the right thing to say, and was concerned if someone was having a bad day. If he discovered that a member of the cast or crew was confronting a difficult personal problem, he would always take the time to give that person a little wave, or his patented cheeky smile, in hopes that he might brighten their outlook.

Sometimes he'd sidle over and tell a joke, just to ease the tension. That kind of effort did not go unnoticed or unappreciated. Talk to anyone who had the pleasure of working with Jack Lemmon, and you will hear story after story of what a wonderful person he was. He concerned himself with others and was the true captain of every ship he sailed, no matter who was actually at the helm. He never allowed all the Hollywood glory he obtained to diminish his inner spirit, and it was that spirit that also made him a fine artist. He often said that he didn't think a great actor could be stupid. I'm sure one could argue that there are some great actors who, while not necessarily stupid, certainly can act stupidly, but Mr. Lemmon's belief was based on the idea that if an actor can reach into himself to understand human nature and portray it with accuracy, how could he fail to lead with that positive outlook in his everyday life as well?

Mr. Lemmon used to begin each take on a film set with the words, "It's magic time." I heard this little phrase, which he would say under his breath, just before the slate was clapped to begin a scene, and I came to realize that it was much more than the simple calling of an artist to his muse

— it was his calling to life itself. With Mr. Lemmon, the entire journey was a magic time, and I am sure that this book will give all of us who loved and admired him a bigger window into that heart that beat so warmly. I still have that photograph that he signed when I was young, and I treasure the inscription: "With my very best wishes always." With Mr. Lemmon, "always" meant "always," and one couldn't have wished for anything better, for he was true to his word and always at his best.

KEVIN SPACEY

Preface

In 1980, my father made a movie called *Tribute*, based on a Broadway play in which he had starred as well. The play was better than the movie, although Pop was outstanding in both, earning a Tony nomination for the play and an Oscar nomination for the movie. The script told the story of a man who is dying of a terminal illness, and of a tribute his friends stage for him. There's also a son in the story, in this case an estranged son.

Fortunately, my father and I had a wonderful relationship. In fact, I adored and idolized Pop. At the same time, however, I knew the real man, the one who lived away from the cameras, and let me tell you, that man was a piece of work. Yes, he was a gifted actor, and yes, he was a fine person, but most important to me, he was a great father and a man who was a hell of a lot of fun to be with — a man who was truly my best friend. There were disagreements, of course, and occasional miscommunications, but I know he never doubted that I loved him with all my heart and soul.

In his final years, even before he was diagnosed with the cancer that ultimately claimed him, Pop was given many tributes by his friends and peers. It was in his final days, though, that I formulated a tribute that I wanted to make to this wonderful father, this "everyman" who won the hearts of moviegoers the world over: I would write our story, all about what he had meant to me, about what it was like to have such a man as my father in my life, about the things we shared, the laughter and the highs, and the occasional hurts and disappointments as well.

I really started out writing this remembrance for myself, and for my children, jotting down a few tales, scenes from our lifetimes together, tales of the "Lemmon Legacy." But as I wrote, it kept growing, and when I mentioned my plan to others who knew him, they wanted to contribute as well, to share their own stories about this memorable, remarkable man.

And so, Pop, this is my tribute, my salute to you. Just as some part of you will always live in the many films you made, just as you will remain an important memory to so many people who loved you as an actor, in the same way you will always live in my heart, and in the memories that I share on these pages.

You showed me magic, Pop.

Acknowledgments

I would like to thank the following people, without whose help and support the stories in this book might have remained slowly fading memories:

Mitchell Waters, Chuck Adams, Elisabeth Scharlatt — respectively the best agent, editor, and publisher I could ever have hoped to have to assist me in putting together this book so close to my heart — and everyone else at Algonquin Books for making the whole experience nothing less than delightful.

Victor Garvey, for being my best friend when I needed a best friend the most.

My wonderful kids, Sydney, Chris Jr., and Jonathan, for making my life a joyous place to be.

My beloved wife, Gina, for putting up with me, and for being the only person on earth who could give me the blessing of being my soul mate.

My dear mother, for loving me like only a mother can.

And Pop . . . for showing me the magic.

Chapter One

THE BIG PICTURE

"Hey, Ramhead, come on over here and give your old man a hug!"

I walked over to the bed where Pop lay, tubes running out of him, connected to the numerous medications that were keeping him alive and somewhat comfortable. He was bald now from the chemo, but his face belied the battle that was raging inside of him. His smile, his beautiful everyman smile, the one the world had adored for over half a century, was still in place. I leaned down and hugged him as hard as I dared.

"What you got working?" I asked, glancing at the TV mounted on the wall across the room.

"Pebble Beach. Jake's doing great, if he keeps this up he's got a real shot!"

I sat next to him and studied his face as he watched the golf tournament that had meant so much to him for so many years, an event he surely would never play in again. I knew it, he knew it, we all knew it, yet he never showed any anger, and his spirits never flagged. He was the bravest man I'd ever met.

During my half-century with Pop, I'd felt just about every emotion a son could feel about his father, from love to hurt, from joy to anger. Over the course of those years I'd done things with him and gone places with him that left me with memories I'll cherish for the rest of my life. And now, as I sat in that hospital room, watching the play of emotions on my father's face, I knew I was about to go through the final experience — saying good-bye.

Cancer has to be one of the toughest ways to go — I knew that; I'd lost my mother to it thirteen years before — but you'd never have known it from Pop. Through it all, I never heard him complain once; all he cared about, his only concern during the final days, was for us, his family. It had been much the same way with my mom, a tough and selfless woman. She'd been told she'd be lucky to live till September at the outside, but she'd wanted more than anything to celebrate one last Christmas, her favorite holiday, with her family, and that's what she did — she passed the day after.

Mom and Pop had fallen in love when they met at New York's Actors Studio many years ago. She was gone now, soon they both would be. And as I did with her, I sat with Pop for the following months and replayed all the movies in my head, all the good times, all the bad, like I was in some huge dream theater. I let that ultimate gift we humans have been bequeathed do its thing — I let the memories open up, and let the film roll . . .

AMERICA'S SWEETHEART

"America's Sweetheart": that's what Pop used to call himself — that, and modest.

He knew how to make an entrance too. His birth in Newton, Massachusetts, on February 8, 1925, had come in the elevator of the Newton-Wellesley hospital. It was reported that he was jaundice-yellow and that one testicle hadn't dropped into place. According to Pop, the nurse who'd been there to do the catching had, on seeing him, puckered her mouth and said, "My goodness, a little yellow Lemmon." They say I also looked like I was from a different planet when I was born, and that Pop took one look at me and asked if he could send me back and get another.

And then virtually the same thing happened to me, a whole lifetime later. Right after my third child was almost born in my car on the way to the hospital, I looked down at him and realized he looked just like Pop, and just like me. And at that moment the whole thing came full circle, and I got the big picture.

The father-son relationship is one of the great mysteries in life — at once intimate, yet guarded; loving, yet competitive. I look at pictures taken of my father with his father, and I see the same look in his eyes that I've felt countless times in mine: a search for approval. Now I see this look coming from my boys as they turn toward me — and the circle grows wider, the big picture more vivid.

It's not just the physical traits that pass from father to son, from generation to generation; I believe that the essence of a father's character passes as well, that it is so deeply embedded in all of us that it will not be denied. I believe my father continues to live in me, just as part of me now lives in my own sons, both physically and spiritually.

Papa Jack, as I used to call my grandfather, was a dapper, successful, and well-liked

Bostonian businessman, with a great sense of humor and a powerful and charismatic personality. At six foot two, he used to barely fit into his sporty convertible, and would ride with his head sticking above the windshield, clutching his bowler hat. I was a child when he passed away, but I remember that when Pop would tell tales of the young Papa Jack, I'd picture my grandfather as one of the Three Stooges, an overgrown Curly Howard, cruising the streets with a "nyuck, nyuck, nyuck." But that image couldn't be less accurate, this guy was no Stooge; he was the real deal, a strong and commanding man.

Not surprisingly, my father's relationship with Papa Jack was complicated, and at its core lay a deep desire for approval — a longing for some indication that he was on the right track; that everything was moving along just fine. Not that this yearning was ever verbalized, not even in the many stories Pop told me over the years about Papa Jack, stories that exemplified that need for approval. No, the dance was much too complicated for that. You could feel those things, but you could never wear your heart on your sleeve, because that's just not what men do, at least not my dad and Papa Jack.

I think Pop was deeply afraid to commit himself completely, emotionally, not only to another person, but also to himself. I think a lot of that fear developed from the formal, Bostonian influence of Papa Jack — a fear of getting too close, because that meant opening up and letting down the walls, and to do that left one vulnerable. Maybe that was why Pop was able to be so charming with just about everyone except those he was closest to — they did not represent a threat.

The relationship Pop and I had was able to go beyond those limitations, especially as I grew older and we grew closer, but for Pop and Papa Jack there would always be that stiffness, despite the deep love underneath it all.

Papa Jack's wife, whom I always knew as GG (short for Gorgeous Grandmother), couldn't have been more different. At barely five feet, she was a pistol of a woman; attractive, intelligent, congenial, and with a terrific sense of humor, she was always the favorite guest at any party. It was from her that Pop got most of the characteristics that made up Jack Lemmon the performer — especially the big, wide, ethereal grin that Pop was so well known for, and which now also can be seen on my youngest boy.

In all the stories he told me about his mother, my father's love for her was quite evident, as was his appreciation for her directness and her sense of humor. Like the time as a kid he'd approached her about the possibility of having a brother or sister, and she'd replied that he must be nuts. "No way I'm going through that again!" she'd retorted. "Once was enough!"

As an only child, Pop had attention lavished on him by both parents, and grew up a loveable kid with a quirky, unpredictable, sweet devil side — the side he got from dear GG, the social belle of the ball, who decreed that after her death she wanted her ashes to be placed in an urn on top of the bar at Boston's Ritz Carlton Hotel. Yes, GG liked to toss them back (as did pretty much the entirety of the Lemmon/Noel lineage as far back as anybody can remember), and like her, Pop loved a good drink and a good party.

Like many of the characters he would go on to play, Pop's personal makeup included a strong dose of the bewildered loser, a quality that endeared him to so many people as he looked at the world with wide-eyed wonder, but a quality that would haunt him off camera as well — especially later in his life, when for thirty-three years running he would attempt to make the cut at the Pebble Beach Golf Tournament, and never succeed.

In Pop, that sense of wonder was coupled with a kind of divine innocence, making him seem relatable and accessible and completely human. This inherent — and to a great extent inherited — quality eventually caused his stardom and earned him his moniker as "The Everyman."

We saw this on display in *Mister Roberts*, when Ensign Pulver blew up his fulminated mercury, and in *The Out-Of-Towners*, when Henry Clark, against all odds, finally conquered the big city, only to be hijacked on his flight back home to Ohio.

Being cast in these roles was no coincidence; these characters were Jack Lemmon from the start. It was a legacy of bumbling bewilderment and vulnerability — the "Lemmon Legacy" — handed down lovingly from father to son, from one generation to another. Like the time Pop almost killed his father, trying to impress him with his throwing arm. He hurled a football at Papa Jack with everything he had, causing his father to run backward, launching himself off the low wall that bordered their property. Needing a trip to the doctor's to get patched up, Papa Jack got into his car and started it, igniting a bag of fireworks my father had hidden under the hood and then forgotten. They almost blew the hood off his prized little convertible and nearly added a heart attack to Papa Jack's list of injuries.

And then there was the day Pop, while playing with the kid next door who'd bragged at what a good woodsman he was, had happily put his foot down on a dare and let the kid take a swing at it with his axe (promising to miss, of course).

Pop walked into the kitchen a couple of minutes later with the entire end of his shoe missing, too scared at first to look at whether the toes had been chopped off with it. Fortunately they hadn't.

The anecdote, though, that most defines my point about the Lemmon Legacy was the one about the time Papa Jack had taken Pop out back to teach him how to safely handle a firecracker. He carefully demonstrated to his young son how to hold the burning lighter in one hand, light the firecracker, then throw the lit fireworks onto the grass, where it would explode. Papa Jack then handed little Jackie the lighter and the firecracker. He watched as Jackie lit the firecracker with the lighter, then threw the lighter on the ground and kept holding the firecracker. According to Pop, they both stood there watching the lighter on the ground with great anticipation, oblivious to the fact that the fuse on the firecracker was burning away in little Jackie's hand. Fortunately Papa Jack realized the situation in the nick of time and managed to bat the explosive away.

The legacy of bewildered bumbling followed Pop through his years at Andover Academy, where he grew from a thin, almost sickly youth into a young man, and it matriculated with him to Harvard University, where one of the truly legendary Lemmon Legacy tales originated. I didn't hear it from Pop; in fact I believe it was our fishing buddy and Pop's fellow alumnus Rick Humphries who told me this story about Pop's first romantic encounter.

The explosion of energy that was my father, especially in his earlier years, was apparently in full display during his college days; add to that some raging hormones and the situation easily could rise to red alert. There was a dance on campus one night, and for the occasion Pop managed to get his hands on a bottle of booze and a hot little blonde. He and the blonde reportedly danced their fair share and drank even more, and by the end of the evening

Pop was a jitterbugging dervish. All the while, of course, the Lemmon smile was beaming and that Lemmon mind scheming.

Evidently the hot little blonde was receptive to Pop's propositions, because without much trouble he managed to talk her into taking a stroll outside, where they found an unlocked car with an inviting front seat.

The car's tight quarters, Pop's inexperience, and an ill-placed stick shift quickly combined to create chaos. Still, youthful passion prevailed as foreplay led to steamy windows that kept the couple obscured until Pop, apparently in an effort to secure his position, managed to thrust his foot through the car's canvas top, where it got stuck.

At that moment he heard approaching footsteps and looked up, no doubt with a perfect Lemmon expression on his face.

"Oh my God, somebody's coming!" he whispered fiercely in the co-ed's ear.

"NOT YET!" she screamed back.

Or at least that's how the story was handed down.

Like Papa Jack before him, while at Harvard, Pop cultivated an active interest in theater. Unlike Papa Jack, though, little Jackie became quite serious about the stage as a possible career, and after college and a brief tour in the navy, Pop set his sights on Broadway. Papa Jack had wanted his son to go into the bakery business with him, and I think it was difficult for him to watch quietly as Pop chose a path other than the one he'd groomed him for. But after heavy soul-searching, Papa Jack finally went to his son and spoke a few eloquent words: "Do what you have to do, but do it because you love it. And remember, I'll always find romance in a loaf of bread."

Papa Jack's words stuck with Pop his whole life, and he said those same words to me, as one day I'll say them to my sons. And so the circle grows ever wider and stronger.

Chapter Two

ALASKA!

The clouds opened up as though a huge dagger had suddenly sliced its way through the sky, and for the first time that week, sunlight spilled onto the snowcapped peaks of the Walatka Mountains. I had a dandy rainbow trout on the end of my fly line doing a tail dance across the ripples of the upper Kulik River, as the zombie fish, seemingly millions thick, bumped against the boots of my waders in the chest-deep water.

And across the river, maybe half a football field away, a six-hundred-pound Alaskan brown bear was hoisting a huge zombie fish, red and green with its vibrant mating colors, up from a deep pool and tossing it to her cubs on the bank. I smiled as I watched the cubs duke it out over the feast, mom relishing her first break of the day, lounging waist deep in the beautiful blue pool. She seemed calm now, but

On our last trip to Alaska, here with a couple of fishing buddies on the Brooks River.

earlier she definitely had been upset with me — and with good reason: I was the idiot who'd unknowingly invaded her space and, more important, disrupted her routine.

I had an excuse, of course. I'd spent the whole week in bed with a killer flu, and finally, on this, the last day of Pop's and my annual Alaskan fishing trip, I'd dragged myself out to the river, getting there just about the time everybody else headed back to the lodge for lunch. I'd declined to join them, and literally only seconds after the twenty-foot aluminum boat carrying Pop, our three fishing buddies, and the guide, turned the corner of the river and slipped out of sight, the hefty momma bear and her two little charges emerged from the Alaskan scrub. She knew the routine, plus this was her lunchtime too. As I watched her, it dawned on me that she was not going to be particularly happy that I'd decided to share mealtime with her — unless, of course, she figured me as part of the meal.

Looking across the turbulent river confirmed my suspicions: she was staring straight at me with definite interest. "Oh great," I said out loud to nobody at all, as I dropped my fly rod, turned, and started shuffling upstream, away from the bear and her cubs. I tried to be nonchalant, but that's not easy to do around an interested bear. After a short hike, I stopped, risked a look back, and saw that things were worse than I thought — the bear had turned and was about to cross the river toward me.

You know the old phrase, "Now you got my attention." Well that definitely applied here. I did the most intelligent thing I could think of: I got the hell out of there, deserting the stream and heading straight into the thick Alaskan bush, which is no simple feat as the thick Alaskan bush is most definitely thick.

And as I stumbled semi-blind through

the gnarly trees and shrubs, I kept thinking to myself, *What the hell am I doing here?* I could be sitting on a beach in Hawaii, or ripping up Paris or London, but instead I'd dropped a bundle of hard-earned cash to end up stumbling through a bear-infested wasteland in the pouring rain after puking my guts out all week long. *Who the hell did I let talk me into something like this?* I asked myself.

Pop, of course. Who else would get me into something like this? I mean, come on, didn't this fit both our MO's? We'd been getting ourselves into this kind of nonsense our whole lives. Wasn't it his idea to come up here for the first time twenty years ago? Sure it was. I remember celebrating my eleventh birthday over at the lodge, when he'd had a huge cake flown in for the occasion — a cake we never got to eat because it ended up in the stomach of a local wolverine.

Yeah, of course. My current predicament was pure Pop. It reminded me of the time he'd hobbled around the corner of the outhouse in search of toilet paper, surprising two elk, mid-hump, and getting himself chased through the middle of camp with his pants around his ankles.

As I stumbled through the undergrowth,

more and more images of Pop came back to me. Twenty years' worth.

And I started to laugh. Standing there, drenched to the bone, covered in mud and in danger of becoming a bear sausage, the memories played upon the silver screen in my head.

RABID RAINBOWS

The rainbow trout of the Tularik River, off of Lake Nonvianuk, Alaska, are without a doubt the most ferocious, Arnold Schwarzenegger–looking *Trogein salmonidae* you ever saw in your entire life. They grow in Nonvianuk and no other place in the world. The reason they grow to their amazing size is because the lake is so big they're convinced it's the ocean.

I'm not exaggerating in any way when I say that I've seen twenty-pound fish pulled out of that river. But unfortunately these very fish I'm speaking about no longer exist, played out through over-fishing, despite the laws that were meant to protect them.

Back in 1974, however, they did. I saw them, and let me tell you, they were truly remarkable. I actually remember one of our guides getting pulled right into the river by a trout that hit his fishing line so hard he just flew.

And on one of those memorable days back in '74, Pop and I and our stolid fishing buddies — Kay Mitsuyoshi, Rick Humphries, and Pete Nestor — had just finished an afternoon of trout stalking and bear avoidance and were lying on our backs on the banks of the Tularik River, listening to Dad tell joke No. 437 for the day.

He was perched on a rock situated over a small waterfall that fell into a beautiful deep pool, and he sat there with a magnificent French bamboo fly rod with gold-plated reel in one hand, and a massive Cuban cigar in the other. We were all relaxing, waiting for the floatplane to pick us up and fly us back to the lodge.

Pop was "on," however, and even after a day that would kill a Sherpa, the punch lines flew, greeted by gales of laughter from the assembled crew.

In the meantime, unbeknownst to my father, one of those huge Tularik leviathans was lurking at the bottom of the pool he was hunkered over, and it had taken an avid interest in the fly at the end of his line. We heard another chuckle from Pop and suddenly he just disappeared. There was a stunned moment of silence on the bank, and then Kay muttered, "There goes another one."

Instantly we were on our feet, searching the river, but there was no sign of Pop. A chill ran up my spine. What was I going to have to tell the world — that Jack Lemmon had been done in by a salmon on steroids?

We ran down the bank, calling his name, and just as I was about to jump in to search for him, I saw my father's hand rising out of the water like a periscope, holding an object above the foam to keep it dry.

It was the cigar, of course. And Pop? He was soggy, but fine . . . Wish I could say the same for that fancy bamboo rod.

Calming down slightly from my initial shock at seeing the bear come after me, I'd doubled back toward my fly rod in an attempt to get my bearings and stay parallel with the river. I was pretty sure (key word "pretty") that Mommy Bear would've finished her banquet and headed out by now, and I was determined not to get too far from home base.

Not being a total wilderness idiot, I called into play twenty years' worth of bush-country experience and was able to make my way safely back to the main river, hoping I'd given the bear enough time to move on. During my nature walk I'd decided that she probably wouldn't have left her cubs unprotected just to go chase me, and I probably would've been safe right where I was, but a little voice in my head had shouted, "Let's not find out!" and I'd listened.

As I stumbled on I could hear ahead of me the rush of the river, and I took comfort that I would soon be coming out of the brambles and brush to a nice, wide-open — and, hopefully, deserted — riverbank.

Unfortunately that was not to be. I stuck my head out of the willows and peered at the other shore. The riverbank was indeed wide open, but it was most assuredly not deserted.

Mommy Bear was directly across the river from me, giving me her sternest bear stare, her two little cubs standing defiantly in the safety of her shadow. One of the cubs snorted, and stamped its paws into the pebbles of the riverbank, and slowly I turned and stumbled back into purgatory, once more trying to remember just how I'd gotten myself into this mess.

PART OF THE PACK

Dogs are pack animals; they do not like having to live alone. Which is why I never understood why someone would buy a dog, and then leave it outside in a doghouse, by itself, later wondering why their dog turned out to be a neurotic mess.

When my mother and father were divorced, I was three years old, way too young for me to even remember what it was like to sit down at the dinner table with them. I'd always idolized and adored my father, and at that young age I couldn't understand why, after a visit, Pop would invariably have to leave and not stay home with Mom and me. It was like my pack was missing its alpha male.

And when Pop went on to remarry and start another family, it created an even greater disparity in my life. My alpha male was gone, Pop had a new family, and as the child of the first marriage, a common casualty of Hollywood divorce, suddenly I felt like I'd been left outside, assigned to the doghouse.

My mother's name was Cynthia Stone. When she and Pop met, they'd both been actors, and despite her own early success — she was nominated for an Emmy — she gave up the business after my sister and I were born. Then, after the divorce, when I was ten years old, we went to live on Santa Monica beach, in Harold Lloyd's great old beach house.

Lloyd, the legendary silent-film star and a dear friend of the family, had rented his house to Mom, and like every house she lived in for the rest of her regrettably short life, in this house there was nothing but joy and love — and parties. At Mom's houses, there were always parties, great parties with great people. And since she and Pop had continued to get along well after their divorce, he was frequently on the scene.

His mother, GG, practically lived with us. She adored Mom and also loved the whole history that Mom and Pop had shared, how they met as young actors on the streets of New York where Pop, fresh out of Harvard, stormed the offices of every agent in town, barging through their closed doors and invariably getting tossed out feetfirst. She loved the work they'd done together on four original television series, and she loved the life they'd started building when they made the move to California. But Hollywood's a tough place, and balance is hard to maintain when there are so many highs and lows. In the end, it had proven to be too much for their marriage.

But the beach house was great, and the parties were second to none, or so they seemed during that era of innocence. Always, though, at the end of those parties, Pop would have to leave and go home — back to a new life, one that didn't include me.

Not much later, Mom decided to marry her old high school sweetheart, who now lived in Florida, and to take my sister and me to live there. He was a great guy, and it meant a great life for our family, but it also meant we would be moving a continent away from everything I'd ever known — and a continent away from my father.

One afternoon before we moved, Pop came by for a visit and a heart-to-heart talk with Mom, and at one point they called me in. Mom looked at me with those incredible eyes of hers, and an expression that made me feel like everything was going to be all right. She asked me if I'd like to go on a trip with Pop.

"Where?" I asked. "Alaska!" she responded. And the following year, 1965, for my eleventh birthday, Pop and I flew to

Anchorage, hopped on a tiny plane, flew another two hours to a little outpost called King Salmon, where we were picked up by an even smaller single-engine floatplane and flown another hour into one of the most amazing wildernesses in the world, the Kenai National Wildlife Refuge.

Everything appears pretty much magical to an eleven-year-old boy who's on an adventure with his father, but this trip was truly special, a visit to a different world. For me, this was the trip of a lifetime, and as the floatplane touched down on the glass-smooth lake in front of the charming small log-cabin town of Brooks River Lodge on that perfect week in 1965, a twenty-year adventure with Pop began.

That first trip went by way too quickly. I was eleven, and I was hanging out with my father. He was mine, all mine — and of course, along with that came the inevitable Lemmon moments.

In just one week, Pop managed to get chased by moose, eagles, and bobcats; he managed to fall in the river pretty much nonstop, sometimes doing a double-header a day, and he managed also to actually get into a full-blown conversation with a couple of bear cubs. This last incident was particularly memorable.

Pretty much every night, there was a poker game in the main lodge, which Pop invariably attended. I was too young to sit in then, of course, but I heard all about them. One night he left the game for his cabin, with fishing buddy Ricky Humphries in tow, along the way telling some kind of wild story involving Rumanian prostitutes. During the story, Ricky, unbeknownst to Pop, veered off the path to visit a local tree, whereupon two bear cubs veered, with perfect timing, right onto the path in Ricky's place. Pop, oblivious to the shift, and still hearing movement behind him, continued on with his story all the way to the door of his cabin, at which point he turned back to Ricky and said, "You're awfully quiet, what's the . . ." He stopped, stared at the two cubs perched on the stairs next to him, who stared back. And after a long beat he said, "Not tonight, I've got a headache," and went into his cabin.

Pop's other great bear encounter that week was, in true Lemmon form, a more public one. As the cabins provided a great view of the lower Brooks River and the path along which each fisherman would travel as he headed back from a day on the stream, the guys who already had returned for the day would usually sit on their porches, clean their gear, and shout insults at the returning anglers. That day Kay, Pete, Ricky, and I were doing just that when we spied the old man of the stream trudging up the path toward camp, as usual, the last one in, and also as usual, preoccupied with straightening out a knot in his line. We shouted and waved hello, he looked up and gave us one of his patented go-fuck-yourself waves, then returned to his knot.

That's when we saw the bear headed down the same path, right toward Pop. We shouted and started waving our arms again; Pop looked up and gave us a yeah-yeah-I-heard-you wave. Then suddenly he and the bear were face-to-face. I don't know who was more startled, Pop or the bear, but Pop screamed at the top of his lungs and turned to run, slipping as he turned and falling face-first into the mud. At the same time the bear turned tail, started to run — and ran headfirst into a tree, hitting it with such an impact that we could hear the bonk all the way up at the cabins. Then the bear just sat back on the ground, dazed and unmoving for a good minute — long enough for Pop to make his getaway.

It was another pratfall, another close call, another day of adventure with my father.

For me, however, the best story — though less exciting — came on the last day of that first Alaska trip. It was a gray and drizzly day, and since our group was pretty much fished out, we decided to stay at camp, pack up, and take it easy.

I'd had such a great time with Pop, though, and now the thought that it was about to be over was getting me down. Pop must have sensed my mood, because at mid-morning he came bounding into the cabin, waking me from a nap.

"Hey, Ramhead! Get your gear on, we're gonna try something new!" And he was out the door. I woke up immediately, excited, and followed him out. One more big adventure loomed on the horizon, and that was just fine by me.

Most of our fishing was done on streams either near the camp, which we walked to, or on beautiful virgin waters that we flew to in the floatplane.

Virtually every day we tried a different spot, but Pop had gotten wind of an area we hadn't tried yet, in a lake called Hundred Island Bay, where a couple of the guides reportedly had trolled from a boat and found monstrous-sized lake trout. Pop, of course, wanted to check it out.

This was quite a few years ago, and the area of Alaska we were in was still pretty much uncharted territory; there were waters we'd fish without knowing what the hell was going to come out of them. And on that final day, we found ourselves in waters just like that.

Pop was the first one to get hit. We never saw what whacked him, but suddenly the tip of his rod just bowed over and the line began to sing off the reel. I thought our little boat was going to flip, but Pop held on, giggling and shouting — until the line went snap, and just like that, it was over.

"What the hell was that?!" Pop yelped, still wide-eyed with excitement. Then he and Roger, our guide, immediately started hypothesizing about what actually could have been at the end of Pop's line. I heard terms like *sturgeon* and *Loch Ness* being bandied about.

Then I noticed a slight twitch on my line, so I slowly lifted the tip. Nothing happened. Then suddenly the line started vanishing from my reel, and just like Pop's, my rod tip bent to touch the water.

I fought the fish as well as a highly excited eleven-year-old kid could, with Pop and

Roger yelling, laughing, and coaching me through the fifteen-minute struggle. Finally we heard the fish break surface. Pop and I hadn't seen it yet, but as we turned to look at Roger, we noticed he'd gotten real quiet.

"What?" I asked. No response from Roger. "What?" Pop asked. Roger whispered in his ear, and then Pop got real quiet too.

"What? What?!" I stammered, reeling against the pull of the behemoth.

Pop leaned over and whispered to me with great sincerity: "It's a rainbow, hot-shot. A biggie. Don't lose it."

Suddenly this was a whole new endeavor. Where only moments before our crew had been joking about thinking we were going to lug up some huge, clunky lake trout, now there was a reverent silence in the boat, as I carefully negotiated the landing of the king of all freshwater fish.

There were two points at which we thought we'd lost the great trout, but finally we pulled it alongside the boat. Roger reached for a net, looked at it, then at Pop, and said, "I don't think it's big enough." Pop replied gravely, "I know you'll do your best, Roger."

And Roger did. With one swoop the prize was in the boat, and all three of us just sat there in silence, staring down at my catch. It did one flip in the hold and the barbless hook fell from its mouth.

After a very long silence, Pop whistled, then said, "That baby could go ten pounds easy."

"Maybe more," Roger replied. "That's the most beautiful 'bow I've ever seen; it'd make a great trophy."

They both looked at me; then Pop said, "Do you want to keep it, kiddo?"

From behind him Roger observed, "It's a gal; she's filled with roe."

I looked down at the fish, barely fitting in the water-filled holding trough at the bottom of the boat. She was the most beautiful rainbow trout I'd ever seen; she would look amazing as a trophy, a memory of this trip, mounted and hanging on a wall. But if left alone, she'd produce a whole bunch more just like her.

I looked up at Pop. He smiled down at me and said, "It's your choice."

That afternoon we cruised through the panoramic finger lakes back toward the lodge, the memory of that incredible experience still fresh in our heads. The rest of the day had been a blast as well, as we went on to catch a bunch of huge lake trout and then release them back into the water. As Pop had said, "We're not here to kill 'em, just piss 'em off a little."

But the highlight was taking that photo, a picture of me and Pop, smiling broadly, both of us holding up the most beautiful rainbow trout we'd ever seen. Then, photo taken, releasing her back into the wild.

The boat turned into Brooks Lake, and I could see the lodge a few miles away. This great moment was the end, the last hurrah, and I knew there wouldn't be another one for a while.

I looked up at Pop: "Can I ask you something, Dad?"

"Anything, kiddo, you know that," he replied.

"How come you and Mom got divorced?"

He thought about my question, then smiled down at me. "I loved your mom, I always will. But we became more like friends than husband and wife."

Then he put his arm around me, and I thought about the week we'd had together — the bears, the laughs, the fishing, the incredible last day . . .

I turned back to him. "Thanks Pop, this has been great."

"For me too, kiddo, for me too."

He paused a moment, then spoke again. "There's something I need you to know."

I looked up into his eyes.

"I'll always be here for you," he said. "You can count on that."

Though I was only eleven, I knew at the time that this was a big father-son moment. I knew he meant what he said — that he'd always be there for me.

And he always was.

And now, here I was, twenty years later, loitering, soaked to the bone in the Alaskan scrub, and I still needed him — him, and maybe the shotgun it would take to get me out of my predicament. The rain had returned, and was really coming down now, pelting the top of my parka as I sat in the middle of a drainage ditch, thirty yards away from the Kulik River and my fly rod. I could still hear the "bear from hell" frolicking in the frigid waters with her two little love-bundles, as I sat there in the middle of the tiny stream, watching the zombie fish roll by.

My ruminations were interrupted, though, by the welcome sound of the big air-horn at camp, signaling that the one-o'clock lunch hour was over.

Hot damn! I thought, Mommy Bear heard that too, and knew instinctively that it was time for her to vanish, because the militia was on the way!

I jumped up and started scrambling through the underbrush, figuring that finally, really, for the first time that week, I was going to get a chance to dip my line into the sacred Alaskan waters.

I came out of the woods right on top of my rod. Excited, I grabbed it, and headed back into the river for my much-delayed meeting with Mr. Trout . . .

And I stopped dead in my tracks. There she was, still tending her cubs, still firmly planted on the other side of the stream, still glaring at me.

Impossible, I thought; this couldn't be happening.

"You're kidding, right?" I yelled at her.

She snorted, pawed the bank, and glared some more. I glared back. Clearly this was going to be a standoff.

Then I turned (not nearly as timidly as I had the first time) and started walking in the opposite direction, muttering to myself that this she-devil of a bear was the most difficult female I'd ever met — and that was saying something for a guy from Hollywood.

I got about ten yards, then stopped.

Something was different; I could sense she wasn't following me. I turned back, and sure enough she was ignoring me completely, actually playing with her cubs in the shallows. I waved my arms; nothing happened. I waved and shouted; still nothing.

And then it hit me — I'd gone in the wrong direction.

It was as simple as that. When Mommy Bear had first come out of the woods and stared me down, marking her territory, I could have gone one of two ways. And if I'd only turned right instead of left when she'd challenged me, there would have been no problem. Ah, choices . . .

I waded into the river and cast my line. Then I turned my gaze skyward and gave the heavens a thumbs-up. In reply, the clouds parted.

Wham! A truly splendid rainbow trout hit my line, jumping and twisting, its brilliant mating colors flashing in the now-sunny reflections of the Kulik River. And as the Walatka peaks lit up, the bear family did their thing, and my gorgeous little rainbow — the last I'd ever catch in these beautiful Alaskan waters — did its thing too, the boat carrying Pop and the rest of the crew rounded the corner and pulled up.

Pop jumped out and jaunted over to where I was reeling in my prize, raised an eyebrow at the ambivalent bears, took a long look at me in my less than pristine state, and barked a laugh.

"Hey, Slick, you look like crap. Havin' fun?"

I smiled back at him. "You bet, Pop — time of my life."

That would be my last fishing trip with Pop. They had been wonderful, memorable — all of them. But time keeps moving, and change is inevitable. Over time, we'd been witness to many of these changes ourselves. In the seventies Alaska hit pay dirt. The massive oil pipeline project split the vast wilderness wide open, in the process transforming the economy as well.

I remember Pop and I used to gauge the astounding rate of growth in Anchorage by the changes in the local strip club, the Great Alaskan Bush Company. In a decade, it had gone from a two-stool bar with one lonely dancer to boobs gone wild.

And over the years, it seemed, as Alaska lost its innocence, so had I. Both of us growing older, coming of age, in the process losing a little bit of the shiny brightness we're all born with. I know that's part of the package; change is an integral part of life, of evolution. But it does come with a price, and because of that, I ask myself: Will I be able to give my two boys what my father gave me?

I believe sincerely that the answer is yes. Alaska remains an incredibly open place, its vast wilderness a tribute to God. And when my own children are ready, I'll be able to take them to that magical place, and we'll create memories together, memories they'll carry for a lifetime and pass on to their children.

But, of course, I can't give them the exact same experience my father gave me. Those times I had with Pop were his and mine, and they happened in a time and place that doesn't exist anymore. Fortunately, while change is inevitable, memories are constant, and the memory of the Alaska that Pop and I knew remains the stuff of a young boy's dreams.

Chapter Three

I lifted myself out of the overstuffed hospital chair that I would get to know so well and walked over to Pop. He was still sleeping. I checked the monitors. His blood pressure was good, but I could see the clockwork drip of the morphine bag as the tube linked to his arm fed the medication to his body. What kind of pain was he really in? I wondered. But, of course, I'd never know; Pop had too much courage, too much strength, and, perhaps, too much pride to ever let us know if he was suffering.

And as I looked down at his face, so vulnerable and honest, a face that had brought joy to millions, a man who had given me such beloved memories, I realized that I needed more time. There were so many things I had left to say to him.

FROM HARVARD TO HOLLYWOOD

Once he had decided on a direction, Jack Lemmon followed his dreams, achieving success fairly rapidly. Not everything had come right away, of course, and as with most artists, the beginning years were tough.

Pop was as proud as he was ambitious, and except for a few loans from Papa Jack when times got tough, he always insisted on making it on his own. He told me many tales about his "fresh-out-of-college-trying-to-make-it-in-the-big-bad-world" years, stories about playing piano at a Manhattan bar called the Old Nick, making a few extra coins by betting that no one could sing "By the Sea" faster than he could. I also remember tales of low-rent, cold-water flats, where he'd have to sleep in the bathtub because that was the only place he was safe from the rats. Those stories, how-ever, as with all such stories by Pop, should be taken with a grain of salt, since all of them could easily be influenced by the "Lilac Lemmon" factor.

By way of explanation, the Lilac Lemmon factor originated with Papa Jack, who was commonly referred to by that name. It came about because when somebody asked him a question to which he didn't know the answer, rather than admit to ignorance, he preferred instead to go ahead and make up an answer. He figured that if the person asking the question didn't know the real answer, they also wouldn't know that his answer was made up. Why this scurrilous behavior was an endless source of joy to him, I'll never know, but I do know that it earned him the moniker Lilac Lemmon, because no one could "lie like Lemmon."

Again, as with so many of the Lemmon legacies I mention, the Lilac Lemmon factor has been handed down lovingly from generation to generation. And with that acknowledgment, I, being of sound Lemmon stock, have offered my disclaimer.

For Pop, the period of the cold-water flat was a brief one. Success arrived, and it arrived in a very big way, bringing with it, unfortunately, its share of problems.

Fame, and especially Hollywood fame, is a jealous mistress. Pop's success came at the expense of his marriage.

He had told me that he and Mom separated because they became more like friends than husband and wife. I know that was what they both wanted me to believe, and I respect that, but in all honesty, I don't buy it. I think that my father's relentless drive to succeed, combined with the sensibilities that were imposed on him by the nature of the business, caused a compulsive self-centeredness that contributed directly to their drifting apart.

In truth, my father was at his happiest when he was working. He was driven to achieve, compelled always to push himself, to make the next one bigger and better. I know that while growing up, I resented his single-sightedness, and I feel that it contributed ultimately to his emotionally short-changing not only those around him, but himself as well. The problem with dedicating oneself body and spirit to work is that, at the end of the day, that's all you have. Yes, the fame is enticing, the money is great, and the awards and adulation are exhilarating, but I don't think Pop ever stepped back to ask himself if these rewards were worth the price of emotional deprivation. I loved the fact that he was a star, but at the same time I wanted him to be more of a father.

He tried, though; I know he did. The trips to Alaska were a great example, and I tend to focus on them because they were the essential thing that Pop did in order to reach out to me when I was young. It was only during those times that I felt he really belonged to me. I know that his true love was his art — it had to be, and that's the way it was. Everything else came second. Fortunately, Pop was sharp enough to recognize his own tendency toward self-centeredness. In an old movie magazine article published when I was seven, there was a picture of him, with a caption that read: "Now divorced, Lemmon says that he'll remarry 'when I can stop concentrating 90 percent on my ego and career.'"

Of course, he did remarry, as did Mom. Pop married a beautiful woman named Felicia, with whom I, unfortunately, never had a particularly close relationship; Mom married an old friend and fellow thespian from the Actors Studio, Cliff Robertson. Cliff was wonderful to have in my life at that time, and to this day remains a second father to me.

Both Mom and Pop did everything they could after the divorce to make it as easy as possible on me. Pop dropped by for occasional visits, always with some kind of gift in hand, and sometimes he'd take me fishing on the day boat out of Santa Monica Pier. He tried, I know, but still there was no denying the void I felt in my life due to his absence. Cliff attempted to fill that void, and did so with great dignity, while always respecting the relationship between me and my father. His care and affection for me continued even after the birth of his own child with Mom, my beloved sister Stephanie.

My life as a kid was basically a good one, but always hanging over me was the separation factor brought about by demon divorce. When they were at their prime and both had remarried, Pop and Walter Matthau, who were true friends off-screen as well as being frequent on-screen costars, took Walter's son, David, and me and enrolled us in a school in the middle of the Arizona desert in a tiny — and then virtually unknown — little town called Sedona.

The school was unique, and I remember those years as being truly a blast. Unfortunately, though, along with the experience came the underlying feeling of being back in the doghouse — a feeling of separation from the pack and, most especially, from my father. Along with that sense of isolation — and despite both Cliff's help and a still-healthy relationship with Pop — came loneliness, accompanied by a struggle for self-identity that would influence the rest of my life.

Chapter Four

JACK LEMMON'S SON

Growing up, the one question I was asked more than any other was what it was like to be Jack Lemmon's son. If you think about it, that's a very strange question for a kid to have to answer. I could respond to people by saying how great Pop was, just as would any other kid who loved his father, but that wouldn't answer the question for them — they wanted more.

When somebody asked Pop a question he didn't want to answer, his pat cop-out line was, "Hello, operator, we've got a bad connection." I had my cop-out lines too, but the real reason I couldn't answer the "Jack Lemmon's son" question was that there were some pretty sensitive issues involved, and that particular question, simple as it was, cut straight to the heart of them, making me feel vulnerable and exposed.

Truth is, from the beginning I struggled with the reality of being a "star's kid." Oh,

At Goldwyn Studios,
coming from Billy Wilder's office.

I was happy with my life, my parents, and my family; I just wasn't overjoyed about the whole "Jack Lemmon's son" thing. Nothing against Pop, of course; I adored him. It's just that going through your entire adolescence identified as an object and not a person can get, well, old: "You're JackLemmon'son? He is my absolute favorite. You tell him I said hello, will you? Did I tell you he was my favorite? George, come over here. You won't believe who this is. This is JackLemmon'son! What was your name again, dear? Oh well, that doesn't matter. You just tell your daddy I love him!"

I remember the first time it really dawned on me who my father was, and by that I mean who he was to everyone else. I was in third grade, attending a small school in Santa Monica. It was recess, and the central courtyard was a buzz of activity. I was attempting to execute just one pull-up on the parallel bar when a red-faced kid came running up to me. "Hey, Lemmonhead!" he said belligerently. "See that kid over there? His father's Robert Conrad. That's the guy who acts Jim West on *The Wild Wild West.* He's more famous than your dad!"

I hung there for a couple of seconds, thinking about what he said, then I shook my head. "Well sure he is, he's Jim West!" And as the kid ran away, I remember thinking, I didn't know my dad was famous; I thought he was just an actor.

I was aware, of course, of the excitement he created wherever he was, although I didn't quite understand it. I remember, as a kid, being out with Pop a number of times and being elbowed out of the way by well-meaning but overly eager fans. During those early years, whenever I was out with Pop, I spent a great deal of time staring at the backs of excited strangers. It was disorienting and confusing, and I didn't always handle it well. It did lead to some humorous situations, though, like the time Pop and I were riding down to the lobby in the elevator at Manhattan's Carlyle Hotel, and a sweet older lady got on at about the thirtieth floor. She spent the next ten floors doing a series of double takes at Pop, then smiled broadly, pointed, and exclaimed, "Jack Lemmon! Alive!"

JackLemmon'son followed me to high school in the red rocks of Sedona, Arizona. By fifteen I was a leather-fringed, love-beaded, granny-glasses-wearing hippie (it was 1969, after all) who had developed a somewhat serious identity problem, a kind of monkey-on-his-back situation.

The years of "object instead of person" had gotten to me, and I had some painful social issues. Whenever I was around people (especially attractive young ladies), I was compelled to come on strong, so that Chris — not JackLemmon'son — could be the center of attention. ("Hey, how are ya! Don't I know you from somewhere?!") In a school of a hundred and twenty students, most of whom had a few issues themselves, this didn't fly too well. As a result, throughout most of my high school years, I was pretty much a social outcast.

JackLemmon'son stayed with me

through my college years as well, but by that point I'd learned a few lessons and gotten some pretty valuable input from friends and mentors, finally coming to realize that I didn't need to live my life solely for the approval of others. I'd calmed down, developed a personality, and was finally coming into my own.

This was also the time when Pop was doing some of his most important work, including the films *Missing, Save the Tiger,* and *The China Syndrome.* Because his career was in high gear, JackLemmon'son activity was at an all-time high, but at least by then I understood what all the fuss was about. For all those JackLemmon'son-ers out there, he was their best friend. He was the guy they invited into their homes or spent a couple hours with at the theater. They knew this man, and they liked him a lot. He was the guy who could make them laugh or make them cry, and he did just what they would do had they been faced with the situations that confronted him — like the loss of a son, or lack of meaning in their lives or, hey, even a nuclear meltdown. He was just like them. They were just like him. And when they met me, they wanted me to let Pop know that they loved him, appreciated who he was, and agreed with everything he did.

Finally, by then, my response was heartfelt and honest: *I will tell him. And thanks, I agree.*

By the time I reached my thirties, I was having a ball. I'd done a load of stage work, starred in a string of TV shows and a number of films, and was enjoying a nice run in a popular TV series. One day around that time, Pop and I were walking through a mall, and people were stopping me for my autograph. For some weird reason, though, no one was hitting on Pop. He put up with this atypical situation, making his usual under-the-breath comments: "Hello, sweetheart, yoo-hoo, over here, big movie star."

When we were alone again, he turned to me and thumped me on the back. "All those years of being Jack Lemmon's kid, and now it's 'Who's the old fart with Chris Lemmon?' "

His remark stopped me in my tracks — all along he'd understood the whole JackLemmon'son thing. But he also had understood that it was one of those things I would have to figure out on my own — this was a life lesson.

I gave him a hug. "You're a great pop," I said, smiling.

He laughed, hugged me back. "Yeah — now pull yourself together, people are talkin'."

Since he's been gone, I've heard JackLemmon'son less and less — when now, of course, I'd finally like to hear it more. I guess that's life.

During his tribute at Pop's funeral, writer Larry Gelbart made a remark that is painfully true: "The Redwoods are falling," he said. And, of course, Pop was one of them, along with Walter, and Gregory Peck, and Katharine Hepburn, and so many others. They were Hollywood's royalty, and now they're gone, and not likely to be replaced.

Fortunately, however, we still have them, as will our children and their children's children. And best of all, we have them forever at their moments of shining glory. We are able to be with them over and over as we watch films like *Save the Tiger*, *The Odd Couple*, *To Kill a Mockingbird*, and *On Golden Pond*. Thanks to the movies, we have them and we always will.

And, incidentally, these days, if someone were to walk up to me and say, "Aren't you, JackLemmon'son?" not only wouldn't I mind, I'd be grateful.

Chapter Five

Pop was awake now, uncomplaining and patient while being poked and prodded by the attending nurses. As I watched him go through this whole ordeal, I never ceased to be amazed at how he maintained his dignity as well as his wonderful — and often bawdy — sense of humor. By now, the nurses were familiar with most of his tried-and-true one-liners, including his own personal favorite, "Wanna sneak a peek at Stiffy?"

"WONDERFUL, JACK, BUT A LITTLE BIT LETH"

Pop's first day of shooting on his first big film, 1954's *It Should Happen to You*, with legendary director George Cukor, found him playing opposite the great actress and comedienne Judy Holliday. As the story goes — one that he delighted in telling —

66

My first Oscar. Yeah, right.

Pop was giving his typically enthusiastic performance, which evidently was a bit too enthusiastic for Mr. Cukor's taste. Speaking with his patented underbite lisp, the director asked Pop to tone it down and give his performance "a little bit leth."

They'd gone through quite a few takes, and after each one Cukor would say, "That's wonderful, marvelouth, Jack, but could you do it a little leth." Another take: "Thplendid, old boy, but pothibly a little leth." Same scene, still another take: "Terrific, but jutht a little bit leth."

Finally Pop had had it, and he yelled, "If I do it any less, I won't be acting!"

To which Cukor yelled back, "Exthactly!"

Pop used to delight in telling stories

about his early days as an actor, usually, as in the Cukor story, with him as the butt of the joke. An especially memorable story came out of something that happened on live television, when he and another actor were portraying detectives — who also happened to be brothers — caught in a perilous shoot-out. The actor in front of him was supposed to get shot, at which point Pop was to fire his pistol, killing the assailant, then grab his injured brother in his arms for a final good-bye.

Unfortunately, in true Lemmon form, Pop had aimed a bit low and fired a fully loaded blank right into his fellow actor's ass. The guy fell back into Pop's arms all right, but he was cursing a blue streak — every word of which spilled out into living rooms all across the country.

On another live TV drama, Pop was playing a doctor in a tense life-or-death operating-room scene, which was to end with the loss of his patient. After a highly dramatic moment, he turned to the nurse next to him and asked for a "hypodeemic nerdle." A long pause ensued, during which the assembled actors pondered Pop's words. Then the nurse started to giggle, and at that point the law of contagious laughter set in, and the anesthesiologist started to lose it, followed by the other two nurses, and before the director could cut away from his collapsing drama, the patient — theoretically out cold — sat up belly-laughing.

Pop also talked about working on *Some Like It Hot*, during which he and Tony Curtis formed a kind of bond (I'm told cross-dressing will do that every time). One story he told about that film happened during (I believe) his and Tony's screen test for director Billy Wilder. Pop turned to Tony and challenged him to attempt the acid test on whether or not their Daphne and Geraldine looks could pass muster. Dragging a bewildered and apparently somewhat hesitant Tony Curtis behind him, Pop led the way to the ladies' room in the lobby of the movie studio, where they then sat and did their makeup for a good half hour. Apparently nobody batted an eye — except, of course, Daphne and Geraldine.

There were many memorable movie moments that Pop liked to recount, but one of the best of his "early days" stories took place on the lot of Paramount Studios and involved the gorgeous Italian actress Virna Lisi. While filming the 1965 feature *How to Murder Your Wife*, Pop had taken a very nasty fall during a stunt, one that could even have been fatal. Fortunately, Pop's quick reflexes had averted tragedy when he grabbed hold of an iron pipe, breaking his fall.

Shaken, he staggered back to the row of identical cottages that served as the cast's dressing rooms and threw open the door to what he thought was his cottage. Barging in, he found Virna Lisi standing naked in front of a full-length mirror, with her incredibly large, muscular, and insanely jealous Italian husband at her side.

Evidently, earlier in the day Lisi's husband had arrived from Italy and proceeded directly to the set, arriving in time to find his wife in the midst of a scene in which she was required to be scantily clad, and in which a number of construction workers were catcalling her. Appalled and enraged, it had taken all of his wife's tact to get her husband back to her dressing room, where she tried to calm him. Apparently she had succeeded — until Pop entered the picture.

Upon seeing Pop (his wife's leading man — the root of his jealousy and the reason for his trans-Atlantic trip) come bursting into his wife's dressing room with, no doubt, a perfect Lemmon leer on his face, the husband could take no more.

Screaming Italian curses, he lit out after Pop. A foot-chase through the Paramount lot ensued, something that, as Pop described it, sounded like a scene out of an old Keystone Kops movie. I'm talking full-out cursing Italian husband, followed by screaming, scantily-clothed Italian actress, followed by grips, producers, and, finally, the director, all of them chasing one scared and badly bruised actor who raced through the studio lot, ducking into every open door and alleyway he could find.

I always enjoyed hearing Pop recount these great old stories, but as funny as they were, I always found the humor ironic as well. As carefree and fun as show biz seems on the surface, once an actor reaches the level my father attained, it puts a hammer-lock on him, basically taking over his life, and that of his family as well.

Egomania is a frequent by-product of stardom — I've seen it destroy many people, even some as intelligent and self-possessed as my father — but I'm happy and proud to say that in Pop's case it was never a factor. Yes, of course, there was stuff he did now and then that would drive me nuts, like the times I'd call him to tell him about something really cool that had

71

happened to me, and he'd start babbling on about himself so much that I couldn't get a word in edgewise, and then, after ten minutes he'd invariably say something like, "Enough about me, what did *you* think of my last film?"

Pop was, in fact, a truly kind and humble man. Walter Matthau called him "a good fellow of splendid instincts and deeds," and that indeed was true. His generous and spontaneous nature came through not only in his films, but also in his life, filling them both with great performances and great times.

I honestly have never heard one person say a bad word about my father. But then I never met Virna Lisi's husband.

Chapter Six

POP'S PORSCHE

My father had a thing for fast, sporty cars, and he indulged his passion by buying one after another. That, to me, was just fine. Pop worked his butt off his whole life, made it on his own; he completely deserved to go out and buy gorgeous — and invariably expensive — hunks of metal if that pleased him. There was only one problem: my father was one of the worst drivers that ever walked (well, actually, that would be drove) the face of the earth.

I loved my father deeply, and respected him completely. When it comes to singing his praises, I am front and center — he was a man of many remarkable talents. Driving, however, was not one of them. In fact, the man couldn't drive worth a damn. Growing up, I saw so many great cars pass through our household it made my head swim. I always related each one with the film Pop was making at the time, because he so easily became the character he was portraying that everything around him seemed to take on that persona as well. This was true especially of the cars.

Between *Mister Roberts*, *Some Like It Hot*, and *The Apartment*, I don't know what he was driving because I was too young, but right around the time of *Days of Wine and Roses*, *Irma la Douce*, and *Under the Yum Yum Tree*, he would come to my school (I believe it was sixth grade) in one of those bubble-looking Jaguar coupés. It was the coolest car around, and all the kids at school would run up, pushing themselves against the fence to get a closer look. I think that particular car met its end when it got backed over the edge of an elevated parking garage.

Then, from the days of *The Great Race*, *How to Murder Your Wife*, and *The Odd Couple*, through *The Out-of-Towners*, *The Front Page*, and *The Prisoner of Second Avenue*, he was driving James Bond's car, the ever-cool Aston Martin. I remember that when Pop would get on the newly constructed Santa Monica Freeway, he'd floor it as he hit the on-ramp, and I would sit there in the passenger seat, just watching the gas gauge go down. I won't even tell you what happened to that baby;

suffice it to say it was a slow and painful death.

The China Syndrome, *Missing*, *Mass Appeal*, and *Dad* found Pop in a vintage fifties MG convertible. I believe that one ended up wrapped around a tree.

Sometime around then I had finished a solid decade of steady work myself (thank you, Lord), and had, after saving up my pennies from each job, decided to take the plunge and test myself to see if I, too, suffered from the Lemmon sports-car curse.

My adventure began one night at a dinner with Blake Edwards and Julie Andrews. (Their clan was like a second family to both Pop and me. In fact, we all did a film together in '86, called *That's Life*. I think Pop was driving a Bentley at the time. It's a shame what happened to that automobile.) Blake and Julie and Pop and some other friends were having dinner with my wife, Gina, and me at our house in the Hollywood Hills. I'd had my eye on Blake's '85 black-on-black, slant-nose Porsche Turbo for quite a while, and after some less-than-subtle predinner wheedling, Blake let me know that he'd be selling the car, and were I interested he would give me a very part-of-the-family price for it.

From across a crowded room of very

funny people telling lots of loud jokes, I saw my father's ears perk up. A moment passed, and then his curious and ever-Lemmon face peered around a corner, taking full note of Blake's and my negotiations. And as he inched forward to view our subsequent handshake, I witnessed one of the truly funniest expressions I ever saw on my father's face. It was a mixture of pride (that I'd worked hard enough to have arrived at a place where I could reward myself), disbelief (that I'd worked hard enough to have arrived at a place where I could reward myself), and downright jealousy (I couldn't have worked *that* hard). I bought the car and ended up driving it for eleven years, loving every minute of it.

But then, immediately following my purchase of the Porsche, strange things started happening. I noticed Pop had stopped meeting me in the driveway when I came to visit at his house. He also wouldn't walk outside with me when I left. Even stranger, when I was inside the house, he would disappear for periods of time and offer no excuse as to where he'd been. Finally, one day I followed him, watching as he sneaked out into the driveway and stood staring at my car with that amazed look on his face.

My father and I always had enjoyed a

good father-son relationship, and, equally important, we always had a great friendship. But now a dark specter had risen over that friendship, and its name was Porsche.

It came as no surprise when I received a call from Pop a short while later:

"Hey, hotshot!" His voice had its usual upbeat tone.

"Hey, Pop, how ya doing?!"

"I don't give out that kind of information. What're you up to tomorrow?"

"About six-two. Why, you want to play golf?"

"No, I want to look at some cars. Pick me up at noon."

From the second I heard his request, I knew what was coming. Sure enough, when I showed up in his driveway the next day, he said, "Why don't we take your car? I'll drive." I knew I was in trouble.

Four misshifts and a throttle burp later, I couldn't stand it anymore, and made him surrender control of the vehicle. Not before, however, he turned to me with wild-eyed excitement, hanging over the steering wheel, yelping, "This car's fast!"

A few weeks later, Pop's very own black-on-black Porsche Turbo showed up in the driveway. On seeing it, I said a silent prayer, knowing that poor car didn't deserve its fate.

In fact, two Porsches and two more Aston Martins bit the dust in the course of *Glengarry Glen Ross*, *Grumpy Old Men*, *Inherit the Wind*, and, finally, *Tuesdays with Morrie*. They were great cars, all of them, and they performed as well as they could under the circumstances.

You see, my father may have been a lousy driver — but man, was he one hell of a good actor.

Chapter Seven

After the nurses had finished with Pop, after he had regaled them with just one more story, after the laughter had finally died down, and we were alone in the room, Pop turned to me. "Hey, Slick," he said, "wanna join me for dinner? Food's not half-bad in this joint!"

I looked at his face — so animated and full of expression, a face that held a million memories — and I was reminded of something a friend of Pop's had once said, that despite his happy face, Jack Lemmon had the saddest eyes she'd ever seen.

EVERYTHING'S COMIN' UP ROSES

Despite all the happiness in Pop's life, despite the awards, accolades, and good times, despite the everything's-comin'-up-roses exterior, it always seemed to me that inside

Jamming in the ocean room
at the beach house.

there was an underlying core of sadness. It showed in his work, when Harry Stoner raged against a meaningless life in *Save the Tiger*, or when Ed Horman failed in his fight against the corrupt and murderous regime that killed his son in *Missing*.

But as with all his other characteristics, that touch of melancholy wasn't just acting, it was in his soul, and as I look back, I begin to realize it was yet another by-product of the Lemmon Legacy.

Pop recognized it in himself, this innate sadness, telling me stories of growing up as an only child, of long lonely walks and afternoons spent in wistful contemplation. I saw it in myself, as well, even as I played my childhood games, by myself, clamoring around the old wooden walls surrounding our beach house, escaping by pretending to be one of my heroes, like Zorro or the Lone Ranger. And looking back, I realize the sadness was there for Papa Jack and GG as well, because despite their great humor and their sense of joie de vivre, they chose to end their lives alone.

For Pop, acting gave him a much-needed outlet, a way to communicate without having to commit. I genuinely believe that my father was deeply scared to commit himself completely, emotionally, to anyone other than those characters he created. The only person I think he ever did commit to totally was Felicia, and I think that was because she represented a battle, a challenge that Pop just couldn't resist — at least until near the end, when I think he just gave up.

When Pop was still at Harvard, Papa Jack and GG had quietly separated. Despite their separation, however, they never officially divorced, and for the rest of their lives never lived more than ten minutes apart. They both moved to Los Angeles to be close to Pop, one living in Brentwood, the other in Westwood. After Pop and Mom's divorce, GG pretty much lived with us at the beach, and Papa Jack would come to visit twice a week, always looking dapper.

He often would take me for an outing, maybe first for a hot dog at the Santa Monica Pier's carousel, then up to the deserted caves above Malibu (which are now wall-to-wall houses), where we'd look for bats. Now, I know looking for bats doesn't sound like the most typical way for a grandparent to spend the day with his five-year-old charge, but then there's never been anything typical about any Lemmon. I thought it was pretty cool myself. But though Papa Jack was great fun and had an adventurous side, I think, in the end, he was lonely.

A couple of years later, at age sixty-two, Papa Jack passed away. All I remember of that time was being taken to the front of the hospital and seeing him wave out the window to me. This was in the early sixties, and they did things a certain way back then: seven-year-olds weren't allowed into those parts of the hospital where people were dying.

So my last image of Papa Jack was of his beaming Lemmon face, bravely smiling even though everything was falling apart. Bravely smiling till the end, just as his son would, forty years later.

After Papa Jack's death, I started to see a lot more of Pop, and as it turned out, his visits opened up a whole other world, one that we'd share for the rest of our lives. Though he loved acting, Pop had a second passion, music, specifically the piano. He had very little formal training, but played by ear, and developed seriously good chops.

The beach house, as mentioned, was rented to Mom by Harold Lloyd (this was directly after her second divorce). It was an enormous (and slightly dilapidated) place, built in the traditional 1920s style, meant for housing and entertaining large groups of people. The place was a treat for a kid to live in.

It boasted an enormous front hall called the Ocean Room, and on his frequent visits to the beach, Pop would sit at our great old grand piano in the Ocean Room and play for hours on end. As with every house Mom ever had, the place took on a welcome feeling, and as a result, no visitor ever wanted to leave; this was true for Pop as well. I think in a life filled with Hollywood nonsense, for him this peaceful spot on the Santa Monica beach was a welcome oasis.

And it really was peaceful — at least until I, at the age of five, decided it would be a great idea if I jumped in on the piano action as well. Though he was patient with my desire to add a pounding accompaniment to everything he'd attempt to play, after a while Pop suggested I take lessons.

It was a fortuitous decision. Over the following years the piano became my first love, and Pop's and my frequent jam sessions together became our second language. It was the piano, ultimately, that helped to heal the rift my parents' divorce had caused, and as the years went by, it was the piano that became the defining catalyst of our friendship. From private late-night jam sessions, to performing together in little nightclubs, or, sometimes, in front of the nation — in good times and in bad times, Pop and I always had the music. Together, we'd always have that.

Five years after Papa Jack's death, we lost GG. It happened suddenly, and it was Pop who found her. It must have been incredibly difficult for him; he was so much like her in so many ways.

Suddenly, a generation of Lemmons had left the stage, and there was Pop and me, front and center. A whole new act was about to begin.

Chapter Eight

Just before Papa Jack died, Pop took him on a tour of Europe. Pop later said that was the time when they finally broke through the stiff Boston-Catholic barriers that had separated them, allowing them to grow closer. I believe it was that trip that inspired Pop to start our annual outings, adventures that helped to forge the deep bond that united us.

These adventures started with trips to Alaska, then moved to the most magical spot I've ever seen, a place where we would share our greatest memories.

PEBBLE BEACH (PART ONE)

Robert Louis Stevenson called it the world's most beautiful meeting of land and sea — or something like that. Actually, I'm not sure it was Robert Louis Stevenson at

At Pebble Beach, joined here by Peter Jacobsen and Andy Bean, the year I turned traitor and made the cut.

all. In fact, I'm not sure it's even a real quote. But it should be, and either way, whoever said it (it wasn't me) was right — California's Pebble Beach is amazing. And it also happens to be home to a number of the world's most spectacular golf courses. The links at Pebble, Spyglass, and Cypress Point are revered around the world. These courses were created by some of the most talented designers in the business, and their astounding grounds are lovingly and meticulously maintained.

And it's precisely their beauty and quality that make me wonder how they ever became the home for the annual Pebble Beach Pro-Am Tournament. Why would they take the world's finest golfers, put them on these incredible courses in this amazingly beautiful place, and mix in some of the world's worst golfers, who just happen to be celebrities? The answer, of course, is to raise money for charity, because without that incentive, I can't imagine a possible justification for such a travesty.

Okay, maybe I'm being a little harsh. The truth is, not only is money raised for a lot of good causes, but most important — at least for the sake of this story — they stage these annual events because they're great fun for everybody — the pros, the celebrities, and the fans — and some of the results are memorable and truly funny.

For those of you who don't know about the Pebble Beach Golf Tournament, it was started by the great crooner and avid golfer Bing Crosby. Over time it grew into a four-day PGA tournament, in which the professionals play all four rounds with some of Hollywood's greatest hackers. And heading up that illustrious group was the king hacker of them all, the crown prince of slice, America's sweetheart and the darling of Pebble Beach — Jack Lemmon.

For thirty-four years running, my father played the Pebble Beach Tournament with only one goal in mind: to make it through the third-round cut and play with the pros on magic Sunday. And for thirty-four consecutive years, through all manner of weather, he trudged and hacked and raged against the elements. And he never once made that cut.

I've been told countless times, by everyone from critics to grocers, that one of the reasons my father was such a beloved personality was his everyman quality. I think that's true, and I think it was never more on display than at Pebble Beach. Year after year, as Pop puffed and struggled his way through seventy-two of the most magnificent holes in golf, he reminded the thousands who watched him of themselves. They related to him, and they rooted for him.

And every year, as the elusive cut slipped away from him, all those spectators felt and shared the agony of his disappointment. They'd watch as he sailed drive after drive into the rocks of Monterey Bay; they'd hold their collective breath as his putts sailed by the cup; they'd clench their jaws as he'd hit the ball into a sand trap, then take enough strokes to bogey a hole without ever reaching the green. They even saw him hang over the hundred-foot beachside cliffs, braving the dizzying drop into the raging Pacific, with Clint Eastwood holding him by the belt so he wouldn't fall.

The gallery watched him as he tried and tried . . . and never quite succeeded. Through it all, they cheered him on, because in Pop they saw themselves, a mirror of their own struggles, their own frustrations. They loved him for being so human, and they responded to his indomitable spirit. They loved him because he kept coming back to Pebble, year after year. They loved him because he never gave up the battle.

I had the great pleasure to be with my father through nine of his Pebble Beach onslaughts, and the stories and memories of those wonderful, magical times are precious to me. These individual recollections, over a period of ten years, make up a big and wonderful picture of my times at Pebble Beach, days spent with America's Sweetheart.

JANUARY 20TH, 1989

I was thirty-four, and at the time was costarring in a popular television series called *Duet,* that aired on a then brand-new TV channel called Fox. The show was actually good, and the whole Fox thing looked like it had legs, looked like it might last. I now had my own career, and with this series it had picked up some momentum, and I was having a ball.

It had been quite a while since Pop and I had been on our annual fishing trip to Alaska, and we both missed the fun we'd shared in those times together. So sometime during the previous September he'd left me a phone message with double his usual exuberance:

"Hey, Ramhead, I got great news! Just got off the phone with Jake." Peter Jacobsen, pop's longtime professional playing partner through his latter Pebble stints, was like a son to Pop, and to this day remains like a brother to me. "You're in, kiddo! You're going to Pebble, and get this — it looks like you might be playing with Mark O'Meara! Only problem is, it's gonna cost you a friggin' fortune. But what the hell do you care, you're in that rotten series, you can afford it!" Click.

Four months later I find myself sitting in a twin-engine Cessna, flying over the beautiful mountains of Big Sur, my father next to me, sound asleep, his head on my shoulder. *Bam!* We hit an air pocket. Dad opens his eyes, looks up at me. "Go fuck yourself," he says. Thus begins the decade-long journey to Pebble Beach.

THIS IS THE YEAR, JACK!

From the minute we touched down at the charming little airport in Monterey, it started — the mantra that would follow Pop for the rest of his days at Pebble: "This is the year, Jack!" Every single person — be they young, old, male, female, black, white, or whatever — every single person who encountered my father had a word of encouragement for him. "This is the year, Jack!" they'd say. I heard that phrase a thousand times: "This is the year!"

Crazy, but in Pop's picture-perfect life, a life with few regrets and so many accomplishments, I think making the cut at Pebble Beach was the one thing he would have appreciated the most. Don't get me wrong; he treasured the two Academy Awards and the flock of Emmys, but to have played on Sunday at Pebble Beach — that would've been the icing on the cake.

So everywhere we went, it was repeated: "This is the year, Jack!" Of course, Pop took the whole thing in his usual stride, marching forward with his Jack Lemmon jaunt, mumbling replies just out of hearing range: "Thank you, thank you very much. Now move aside, please, golf-biggie coming through."

On my first trip to Pebble, I wasn't sure what to expect, and as the car turned the corner onto the bluffs above Carmel, I took one look down at the lodge and the crown jewel itself, Pebble Beach Golf Links, and was truly speechless. (Yes, it's true; there actually are ways to silence a Lemmon.) I was so dazzled I barely heard Pop when he chimed up next to me, "Crappy view, huh?"

We entered that magical valley, riding the narrow lanes past the gorgeous Mexican villas, and finally arrived in the central courtyard of the lodge. We looked over at the practice putting green and saw Tom Watson in a putt-off with Jack Nicklaus, while Fuzzy Zeller tossed barbs at them from the sidelines — it was all so amazing. Was it possible that I was here for a whole week, a week in heaven, with the greatest tour-guide a guy could ask for, "The Hinge"?

"The Human Hinge" was the nickname Peter Jacobsen had given my father the first time he saw his golf swing. Though typically used to describe a swing that was less than poetic, Pop's interpretation was that the moniker stood for poetry in motion. In actuality, Pop's approach to the ball began with a routine that could launch a sitcom, as he repeatedly removed from his mouth, and then brandished, his ever-present oversized Cuban cigar, which he would finally hurtle to the ground as he began his backswing. The swing continued with a quick turn of the body, a blur of the wrists, a splay-footed finish, and his inevitable war cry, always delivered at the top of his lungs: "It's a piece of *shiiiiit* . . ."

We checked in at the lodge (Pop was right: this was going to cost me a fortune), had lunch, hit the rooms, unpacked, and the next thing I knew I was standing on the first tee of the world-famous Pebble Beach Golf Links.

There are no golf carts allowed on the course at a pro tournament, so, like the pros, we amateurs had to find a caddy to carry our bag through the four days of play. Picking the right caddy is extremely important because you have to find someone who knows the course and can help your game, but it must also be someone with a good personality, someone who'll fit well into the rest of the foursome of players and their caddies. However, most important, for the pro's sake, an amateur must pick a caddy with a cheerful and professional demeanor.

I didn't do any of those things.

Pop had a crazy character named Dove Christopher carrying for him. (And in later years, he would wrangle golf guru Dave Pelz into lugging his two-ton bag around the course; unfortunately, even that didn't help his game.)

Out of desperation, I ended up hiring an inebriated Scottish giant who barely spoke the same English as I did. His name was Angus, and while he never did really help me with my game, we formed a weird kind of bond. In fact, not only did he carry my bag that year, he carried it for many more as well. And during that whole time, the only intelligible words I heard from him came every afternoon at the end of the round, when he'd saunter up to me and say, "That'll be a hundred dollars."

But while I may have gotten used to Angus, I never really got used to the excitement of playing Pebble, and I remember the first time as being something of a religious experience. Pop was playing really well that day, and we were all jazzed about his chances for the tournament, now just two days away and looming large.

That night Pop and I had dinner at what became our hangout, the Grill

Room. We were just finishing up when Jake flew in, brimming with his always-contagious enthusiasm.

"Get this, you guys! Chris is in the scramble tomorrow!"

"What?!" My old man almost choked on his chocolate shake. "How'd the rotten bastard get in there? Couldn't be that crappy series he's in."

Jake sat down and slapped me on the shoulder. "He's in! It's gonna be Clint, Glen Campbell, Mark McGwire, Alice Cooper, you, and Chris!"

"There's no accounting for taste!" Pop turned and beamed at me.

"What the hell are you guys talking about?" I asked.

Jake and Pop looked at each other, burst out laughing, then turned back to me with Cheshire cat grins.

"You'll see," Pop said, and clapped me on the back.

THE CELEBRITY SCRAMBLE

I was standing on the first tee at the Pebble Beach Golf Links, literally staring down a human tunnel. There were at least a thousand people gathered in the gallery, lining both sides of the fairway, and it felt like they were all staring at me — which was okay, since, being a Lemmon, I loved performing for a crowd. The problem, however, was that they were lined up in what I call "pro style," leaving me no margin for error in getting the ball off the tee. Such intimacy is fine for the pros, but for a hacker like myself — someone who's been known on occasion to actually miss the fairway — the fact that I'd have to nail it through a virtual living telescope was a bit daunting.

Seeing my dismay, champion golfer Nick Faldo strolled by and clapped me on the back. "Don't let it get to you, Chris. We hit 'em all the time. Calchavechia laid some guy's head open the other day. You get used to it after a while."

Nick split and Jake walked up: "Don't listen to Faldo; he's partnered with Alice Cooper this week. He's just gaming you." He slapped me on the back and walked away.

Pop walked up and put his arm around me. "Good luck, kiddo. Watch out for that trap on the left."

Et tu, *Papa?* I thought. My own father was gaming me, and with the oldest one in the books. "Watch out for that trap on the left," he warns, so that while you're teeing up, all you can think about is the goddamn trap on the left.

Before we tee off, though, I should back up for a second and explain what the Celebrity Scramble is, and why the competition is so fierce that a loving father would try to place his own son's drive in "the trap on the left."

As was the tradition, every year, on the day before the big tournament, there was always a five-hole mini-tournament played by six celebrities who were lucky enough to be chosen out of the field. I say "lucky," because playing in the scramble was a highly coveted honor. There were certain legendary Pebble players who were shoo-ins to play the scramble every year, among them Clint Eastwood, my father, and a few others. But sometimes there were also young maverick celebs who got a chance, especially if the field of established stars happened to be thin that particular year. This year those coveted "maverick" spots went to Mark McGwire and myself. (Remember that this was 1989, and though Mark had already made a name for himself, he hadn't yet turned into the baseball superstar he would become just a couple of years later.)

The rules of the scramble were simple: six guys play five holes; high scores are eliminated at each hole; the last one standing wins. And let me tell you something: there might have been plenty of playful ribbing, gaming, and joking going on among our little group, but if you don't think that every last one of us was there to win that day, then you sorely underestimate the competitive nature of a celebrity. Like the tournament itself, on the surface, the scramble was all fun and frivolity, but also like the tournament, at its heart, it was deeply serious stuff.

That February day in 1989 was my trial by fire. That was why Pop and Peter had given me those huge grins at dinner the night before. They already knew only too well what I've come to call the "Pebble Factor." Basically, it goes something like this: "Have a great time, kiddo. But play your heart out, 'cause this is the real deal. Oh, and watch out for that trap on the left."

I was the last of the celebs to tee off, and I somehow found the guts to yank my virgin butt up onto the tee, right in front of Clint Eastwood, Alice Cooper, and the world, and not to pass out when the announcer called, "And now, from Hollywood, California. Ladies and gentlemen, actor Chris Lemmon!"

I'm pretty sure I closed my eyes when I hit that first drive, but amazingly, when I was finally able to unsquint, I spotted my ball tracking a gentle fade around the eucalyptus trees lining the right side of the fairway, and settling down at a lovely spot for my approach to the first green. The gallery applauded as I stared in wonder at my accomplishment, then everyone started moving down the fairway. I was still posed on the tee, staring in wonder, when Pop came up behind me, smacked me on the ass, and said, "Great drive, kiddo. Now knock it off."

The first hole saw Glen Campbell fall by the wayside, and on the second, the legend of Carmel, the coolest guy in the world, Mayor Clint Eastwood, said good-bye. Alice Cooper was gone on three, and that left Mark McGwire and two guys named Lemmon to play the final two holes, seventeen and eighteen.

I noticed Pop giving McGwire a furtive glance as he addressed the ball on the seventeenth tee. I'd seen that look from him before, up in Alaska, when a grizzly bear started getting a little too close.

Unfortunately, Pop was the next to fall,

and I thank God it wasn't me he fell to —
I'd never have been able to live with that,
and you can bet your sweet patootie that
Pop wouldn't let me live with it either. He
fell to McGwire, and though I truly wish it
had been him walking down the eighteenth
fairway instead of me that day, I am truly
thankful that at least it wasn't him against
me.

The last hole of the scramble found
home-run-hitting Mark McGwire going
face-to-face with *moi*. There was a coin toss.
Mark got the honors to tee off first, and as
he got ready to hit his drive, Pop sidled
over to me with that grizzly-bear look in
his eyes and whispered, "Big sonofabitch,
isn't he?"

"Pop, you're out of the scramble and
you're still gamin' me?"

"Who's gaming?" he shot back. "I'm just
making an observation — that he's one
very big sonofabitch."

I turned and looked out at the magnificent eighteenth hole, a 543-yard master-
piece that gently arcs around the royal-
blue waters of Stillwater Cove. Here I was,
with my beloved father, about to tee off
against Mark Friggin' McGwire in the
final hole of the Pebble Beach Celebrity
Scramble.

And that's when Mark took a mighty swing and dead-croaked the ball off the heel of his club and straight into those royal-blue waters of Stillwater Cove. My old man immediately whispered, "You just won."

And then, equally unbelievably, McGwire's golf ball hit one of the few rocky teeth that jutted up out of the water, ricocheted, and landed smack-dab back in the middle of the fairway. My old man immediately whispered, "You just lost."

McGwire turned to the gallery and made an exaggerated gesture of wiping the sweat off his brow, and then it was up to me. I walked up to Angus who handed me my driver.

"Any suggestions?" I asked.

"Take up tennis," he mumbled.

Despite the nerves, I was able to get a decent, although lackluster, drive out into the fairway, and the game was on.

McGwire walked the hundred-fifty yards to where his ball had landed and pulled out a three-iron. He then hit the most beautiful three-iron shot I've ever seen. And as I stood watching that ball etch the gentle coastline of Stillwater Cove, I got fired up. Hellfire and boy-howdy, I thought, this is the real deal; now let's rock 'n' roll! And so we did, as Mark McGwire and I went *mano a mano,* take-no-prisoners, nose-to-nose, down one of the world's most famous fairways.

As though in a dream, I seem to remember Pop saying he was there to advise me, and Jake saying, yeah, just listen to him and do the exact opposite, and then the whole thing was just a big blur, ending with McGwire and me on the eighteenth green, each of us there in four, both of us with long putts for par.

The gallery was on its feet. Pop and Jake were just about doing the jitterbug on the side of the green, with Pop waving emphatically and mouthing instructions: "It breaks right, it breaks right!" Jake was behind him, gesturing even more emphatically: "It breaks left, it breaks left!"

I didn't care what they said; I just shut my eyes and swung.

I rimmed the hole from about thirty feet out, and thankfully had a tap-in for bogey, even though anyone who's played Pebble will tell you there's no such thing as a tap-in on that course. And then it was McGwire with a twenty-footer for the win. He struck the ball perfectly; it was a truly beautiful putt, but it didn't fall.

Though he observed perfect decorum, and didn't actually utter a sound, I could hear Pop's inner voice scream, "Yee-hah!"

loud enough to shake the hills.

I turned and looked at him. Everything was happening in slow motion: McGwire shaking his head, tapping in his bogey; the gallery jumping up and down, screaming; the sea-gulls circling overhead; Pop, standing on the side of the green, beaming. I walked over and gave him a hug, and he looked me in the eye and said, "Welcome to Pebble Beach."

I think Pop always knew how much I valued those trips with him, the ones to Alaska, and then to Pebble Beach. I know he knew how much fun we had together. We had run from bears together, fallen in streams together, and now we'd walked hallowed fairways together — but that day, to do what I'd done, to be where I'd been, and then to see that look of pride on his face, that was the ultimate prize, one of the greatest gifts of my life.

Mark ended up winning the scramble in a close chip-off, which was cool — Mark's a great guy, and just by being there, part of the final action, Pop and I had already won anyway.

And honestly, losing really doesn't look all that bad when you're losing to Mark McGwire, now does it?

Chapter Nine

After Pop first spent some time in the hospital, there was a reprieve, a temporary retreat by the cancer that had attacked him. I credited his tough Lemmon stock for giving him the strength to fight back successfully. Afterward he'd gone home and I'd gone back to my family in New England, thrilled that he was doing so well, and excited to be starting production on my new film.

But then, only a few short months later, I'd gotten the call that had me flying back to California. The cancer had come back, vigorously, and Pop had to undergo a whole new round of operations. When I arrived in Los Angeles, I went directly to the hospital, back to the same room he'd been in before. As always, everyone at the USC/Norris Comprehensive Cancer Clinic had done a top-notch job, and what with the chemo and the radiation, there was still hope, still a slight chance for recovery —

or so I kept telling myself.

As I'd done so many times before, upon reaching his room, I sat next to the bed and looked down at his sleeping face. He awoke once that night and started to sit up, but then winced, touched his tummy, mouthed the word "Ow," and slipped back to sleep. Even that simple exclamation revealed a wealth of information about the kind of man he was. In his little "Ow" there was no anger or self-pity — it was more as if he was simply surprised at this painful inconvenience.

I'd smiled when he'd done it — as always, surprised at his reservoir of strength, in awe of how, even in these terrible circumstances, he was still a class act. Pop pretty much raised the bar in whatever he did, including displaying a sense of decency that brought all around him up a level. It was one of his qualities that I valued most, and I'd always tried my best to emulate it. So here, even undergoing these trials, even on this road to the inevitable end, he was still teaching me lessons.

TAKE TWO

Papa Jack had passed away while Pop was shooting *Days of Wine and Roses*, the film that gave my father credibility as a dramatic actor and allowed him the artistic flexibility afterward to pursue pretty much any role he wanted. Having been labeled solely a comedic actor up to that point, *Days* had finally shown Jack Lemmon's incredible versatility. It also cemented a bond between Pop and writer-director Blake Edwards, establishing a relationship that spanned three films and forty years of friendship.

In *Days*, for the first time, he demonstrated his astounding talent for drama, and if there was any one moment in the film that made the viewer aware of his dramatic range, it was the famous greenhouse scene in which Pop's character, Joe Clay, destroys a plant-filled greenhouse while fruitlessly searching for his hidden bottle of booze.

Pop told me that the scene was so physically and emotionally demanding that he went straight home after wrapping and immediately got into bed, where he slept like a rock — with a big smile on his face. I remember him saying he thought it was the best work he'd ever done.

When he showed up at the studio the next morning, however, he found the entire set had been rebuilt. As he stood staring in amazement at the brand-new greenhouse, not one person, crew member or production staff, even made eye contact with him. Finally Blake Edwards came up from behind and put a hand on his shoulder. "They lost the footage in the lab last night, Jack," he said. "We've got to shoot it again." Pop said he didn't do the scene as well the second time, but having now watched that movie more times than I can remember, all I can say is, that first take must have been a humdinger.

Of course, unlike the greenhouse scene, there are no second takes in life, and that holds for career choices as well. As an actor, once you've committed to a project, you're stuck with it, from the first day of preproduction through countless generations of critics for years and years to come.

Picking the right project is a daunting task for actors, often equal to, if not more important than, the performance they'll eventually give. My father loved his craft and had great respect for the art behind the business, which showed in everything he did, and he had an uncanny ability to consistently make the right choices throughout his career, something that is not easily done. My mother used to say that when he was first starting out he would spend months working in his rose garden while turning down roles — high-paying jobs — that he felt weren't the right creative choice for him at the time. And with noticeably few exceptions, he guided his career as well as any actor I know.

Of course, there were a few notorious misjudgments, like the 1976 film *Alex & the Gypsy*, one of his, shall we say, less inspired choices. Pop invited Walter Matthau to a screening of the film, and afterward he and Walter continued to sit in the theater as the audience quietly filed out (quiet after a screening is never a good sign). After a long pause, Pop turned to Walter and nervously sputtered, in his famous Jack Lemmon stammer, "So, uh-be-de, whadd'ya think?" Walter pondered the question a moment and then answered, "Get out of it."

Fortunately, though, most often Pop was blessed with great foresight and a remarkable "ear" for making the right artistic decisions, even if it meant great personal sacrifice. His first loyalty was always to the project, a difficult thing to maintain when you've achieved the level of fame he did and are constantly being reminded of your importance. This quality made him a very popular actor to work with, and helped to keep him in demand. The producers, the directors, everyone knew that Pop's ability to place his ego second to his art resulted in a better project and eventually a more artistically sound and profitable film. Indeed, Jack Lemmon was smart.

A classic example of Pop's selflessness was his decision to turn down a part that he knew had Academy Award potential, and that he believed he could play well, but which he also felt someone else was more appropriate for. Because he was so impressed with the project, though, he ended up coproducing it. Thus, in 1967, instead of casting himself in the lead role, he went with his hunch and approached Paul Newman. And indeed, Mr. Newman was nominated for an Academy Award in 1967 for his portrayal of Lucas Jackson in *Cool Hand Luke.* No doubt it would have been a memorable film anyway, but Pop's uncanny instincts and his willingness to do what was best for the project helped produce a brilliant film.

I can enjoy watching just about any of Pop's films, although some are special favorites for me. As a child, I occasionally visited him on the set, and in that context the film that I remember most fondly is *The Great Race*, in which Pop starred with Natalie Wood and Tony Curtis. I think, despite the "firehouse" aspects of the film, it was one of my father's great comedic performances, especially (he played multiple roles) as the Prince of Potsdorf. Blake Edwards always wanted to make a sequel to that film, but wasn't able to wrest the rights away from Warner Bros. Years later, during the filming of *That's Life*, he approached Pop and me with the idea that we do a remake in which the character Professor Fate had a son (me), and the Prince of Potsdorf had twin sons (me twice). I would have given anything to have made that film, but it was not to be.

My other favorites of Pop's films include his performance as Ensign Pulver in *Mister Roberts* (an easy choice — a great performance in a great film), *The Apartment*, *Irma La Douce*, *The Odd Couple*, *The Out-of-Towners* (a truly stellar comedic performance), and more recently his ensemble work in *Glengarry Glen Ross* and his incredibly touching turn in *Tuesdays with Morrie*.

As for which were Pop's favorite movies, I can say with authority that he was proud of both his Oscars (*Mister Roberts* and *Save the Tiger*), but he was most proud, I think, of the two controversial (at least at the time) "issue" films he did, *Missing* and

China Syndrome. I know that both these movies reflected his own personal beliefs, and I think Pop viewed *Missing* as especially important. His performance in that film has taken on special importance to me because of a conversation Pop had with my wife, Gina, in which he revealed that while filming he used me as the image for the missing son. He never told me that, which points up an interesting trait in our relationship — there were never many compliments (or criticisms for that matter) from Pop that came to me directly. So when I heard that from Gina, it touched me deeply.

In the theater as well, Pop's choices often weren't easy ones, sending him to Broadway to appear in plays like *Tribute, Juno and the Paycock*, and a highly acclaimed revival of *Long Day's Journey into Night.*

Of course there had also been a less well-remembered play titled *Face of a Hero*, for which Pop received the handle "Trace of a Zero" from one of the reviewing critics.

But hey, just as the Joe E. Brown character says in *Some Like It Hot* when Pop, as Daphne, rips off his wig and announces that he can't marry him because he's not even a girl, "nobody's perfect."

Chapter Ten

POODLE PATROL

Nineteen seventy five was truly a remarkable year, on many fronts: Jack Nicholson won Best Actor for his performance in *One Flew Over the Cuckoo's Nest*, Elton John was on the radio singing "Philadelphia Freedom," the war in Vietnam was finally over, and I'd just turned twenty-one (undoubtedly the major event of the season).

Naturally, along with my coming of age, there came a lot of unanswered questions, worries, and concerns. Ever since my introduction to the piano, at age five, my whole life-plan had been to become a classical pianist. However, in one fell swoop, that dream had hit the old wall of reality, and I'd received what I like to call "the hot kiss at the end of the wet fist." I didn't have what it took to make it in that field, a realization I'd come to just in the nick of time. Unfortunately, that meant that I had to fall back on plan B — a career in acting.

And since I was about to launch myself into a profession that would pretty much have me following in King Kong's footsteps, it's easy to understand why I might have a question or two.

When I was a kid, Pop had told me that he'd always be there for me, and he always had been. So when I went to him for some adult advice, he took me out to dinner at our favorite spot. He ordered us a terrific meal and a couple of excellent bottles of Chianti, during the enjoyment of which we had great conversation, and, of course, more than a few good laughs. Once back at Pop's house, with my stomach full of calamari and red wine, I started feeling much better. And as we sat at the bar, mulling over the complexities of life and testing certain varieties of very fine brandy, that feeling of wellness just kept growing. By the time we made it to the piano for our inevitable jam session I was feeling downright euphoric. Troubled world? What troubled world?

That's when Pop's housekeeper came bustling into the room, red-faced and flustered, yelping that we'd left the front door open and the two dogs (French poodles named Walter — yes, after that Walter — and Virgil — I'm less certain where that name came from) had flown the coop.

A quick fade-out/fade-in found Pop and me diligently searching the deserted back streets of Beverly Hills, Pop creeping along in his thunderously large old Mercedes 600, me sitting on the hood calling, "Walter . . . Virgil . . ."

We passed more than one cop that night, but they looked the other way; even L.A.'s finest weren't up to the task of mixing with the Lemmon boys. Having little success in our search, we decided the prudent move would be to head back to Pop's bar and weigh our options. And that's when it hit us: Coburn! Jimmy Coburn! That's where the little devils were! That's where they went every time they got out! Another fade-out/fade-in found us wandering the yard of Pop's next-door neighbor, home of fine actor and fine fellow James Coburn.

We tiptoed about, calling for Walter and Virgil in that slurred, overly loud whisper typical of someone in our slightly inebriated state. Stumbling through Coburn's beautiful gardens, and wading through his koi pools, we paused for a moment to take a gander at the terrific view of the city his property afforded.

Suddenly we both froze. There, before us, like two specters of misbehavior in the evening fog, stood Walter and Virgil. We didn't dare move; we knew the second they saw us they'd be off and the chase would be on in earnest. Standard French poodles in their prime are nothing to be toyed with under the best of circumstances, and those two were certainly more than a match for us that evening.

Softly, ever so softly, my father broke the silence, using a voice that had been trained over the years to soothe even the most savage Hollywood beast. He whispered, "Virgil?"

Instantly both dogs' heads snapped around, recognition written all over their fuzzy faces. In a flash they were off! It was a mismatch from the start, of course: two drunken actors chasing two feisty poodles who had no intention of ever letting us catch them.

The end of the chase found Pop and me panting, exhausted, wet, dirty, and disheveled, standing in front of the huge picture window in Jimmy Coburn's bedroom.

Bent over, catching our breath, Pop put his hand on my shoulder and turned to me. "The little shitheads can move, can't they?"

"Never seen anything like it, Pop," I replied.

He leaned over, his breath foggy in the cool morning air. "Ya know what?"

"What?" I said.

He wobbled, caught his balance. "I think somebody's watching us."

Slowly we turned and looked back at the big picture window, and there stood Mr. James Coburn himself, a floor-length robe covering his six-and-a-half-foot frame, a frown creasing his impressive face.

A long moment passed. I think Walter and Virgil may have even done a quick run-by behind us, as we just stood staring at James Coburn. And then in typical Lemmon Boys style, Pop and I pointed at each other in unison and yelled, "He did it!"

Oh yeah, and about the advice Pop gave me that night?

Don't be so hard on yourself . . . Go with dachshunds.

In truth, though, I think Pop really was reluctant to try to give me a direct leg up in getting started because he feared the old nepotism bugaboo. Actually, it's odd when you think about it: in just about any other business, when a son successfully follows in his father's footsteps, he's considered "a chip off the old block," but in show business, the first word that comes to mind is "nepotism," and that was something my father was afraid of. Still, when I went to him for advice on how to approach a role I was to audition for, I sometimes couldn't get him to shut up — he was instantly on his feet, digging into the character, helping me find the right interpretation.

I think it was a very honest and responsible choice on his part, allowing me to find my own path artistically, yet being there, ready to jump in and help me with my craft whenever I came to him as a fellow actor.

The man was truly a piece of work.

THE CHLOE CHRONICLE

As for Walter and Virgil, the canine scourge of the 90210, they ran their races through the seventies and into the eighties, until Father Time caught up with them for good. And I've got to say, despite their obnoxiousness, it was kind of sad to see it happen.

Of course, before we reached that point, there were many more midnight chases for Pop and me, although, toward the end, their little doggie hearts didn't seem really to be in it, and finding them wasn't the same nearly impossible endeavor.

And, when we did find them, lumbering down the street, bumping into each other in a desperate attempt to muster the energy once again to spread terror through the neighborhood, all we had to do was open the car door, and, with looks of resignation in their coal-black eyes, they'd lower their heads and clamber in. Chase over.

Such is our legacy, both for man and for his best friend. In the end, Father Time will catch us all. Walter and Virgil had a great run, so to speak, before moving on to terrorize higher places. And then, after a sufficient period of mourning, they were replaced by a pooch nonpareil, the queen of all canines — and she knew it only too well — Chloe.

Let me paint a picture of Chloe for you: This was a dog whose water bowl could only contain Evian with ice cubes — who insisted on riding in the front seat of my father's Aston Martin, even if there were other people in the car — who would only fly first class, and would get very mopey if it wasn't Air France. This was Lady Chloe, my father's little princess, a pooch who endured until Pop's untimely end.

Like Walter and Vigil, Chloe was a truly fine black standard French poodle, with an aristocratic pedigree. She was the apple of

Pop's eye, and as dogs will when their masters grow older, she filled a place that needed filling in his life.

Unlike Walter and Virgil, Chloe didn't run amok at the first sign of an open door, but in her own special way, this little girl led Pop on an even merrier chase, and she had Pop right in the palm of her, well, paw the whole time. At heart, Chloe was a very sweet dog, but like a lot of other standard poodles, she had this intense way of looking at you that made you think she was about to explode, to just go up in a big ball of flames. I even found myself edging away from her at times, thinking — sixty pounds of dog, up in smoke, move away. That was Chloe, and for the rest of his life, she was who Pop had with him, wherever he went, all the time.

I wasn't exaggerating when I said that Chloe flew in jet planes, right along with the passengers. I swear to you that Pop was able to spin it so Chloe could march onto a plane, straight to the first-class cabin, sit herself in her fully paid for full-fare seat, and kick back.

She would also accompany Pop to the set whenever he was shooting. Once there, she delighted in running around after the grips and nipping at their tool belts, something that no dog should do lightly. Yet she did it with such aplomb that she got away with it, thanks in no small part to her terrific sense of humor.

Chloe even went along with Pop on his Mr.-Toad's-Wild-Ride-in-his-son's-Porsche-grinding-till-there-are-no-gears-left excursion, though that time she was smart enough to sit in the backseat.

My favorite Chloe story of all, though, was when Pop showed up for a meeting on a project of mine he'd taken an interest in — a meeting with then chairman of Paramount Pictures, Sherry Lansing — and he showed up with . . . guess who . . .

It was pouring rain when Pop drove onto the Paramount lot in that week's vehicle (which I believe was a spanky little Ferrari that would very shortly become scrap metal). He pulled up, splashing water on me, then threw open the passenger door, releasing Chloe into knee-deep puddles.

He strutted over to me. "Hey, hotshot — ready to wow 'em?"

I looked down. "Pop . . . You brought Chloe?"

"Absolutely! Somebody's gotta close the deal!"

Chloe joined us, soaking wet, in Sherry Lansing's office, dripping all over the silk-upholstered furniture. I can only thank the Lord that Sherry Lansing is one of the nicest people on earth, since I can still find gainful employment on the Paramount lot.

Chloe's reign continued through the early stages of Pop's illness and even beyond, although, alas, she was not allowed to visit him at the hospital. A year after Pop died, Chloe died as well, and in truth, I don't think she ever recovered from his loss.

I hope that somewhere up there in the heavens there is a big, luxurious 747 with the two of them ensconced in first class, with Pop doing his crosswords — an obsession of his — and Chloe doing whatever the hell it is a dog does in first class. It's a wonderful image, and I'm sure that very odd couple is having a ball.

Chapter Eleven

I'd been pulled away from Pop's side by a call on my cell phone, and, as always, I walked out to the courtyard in front of the hospital to retrieve it. Somehow, answering the inescapable pull of everyday life, in this place where infinitely more important things were at stake, just didn't seem right.

The conversation over, I walked back to the room. It had been a day since his surgery, and the doctors felt confident that he would come around soon. But when I returned, he was still asleep, and with a smile on his face — who else but Pop?

"A STROLL IN THE PARK"

". . . with my little duckies!" My mom loved saying that, and loved being in New York and walking through Central Park on a beautiful spring day in 1988, accompanied by her two "little duckies," as she called my sister Stephanie and me.

I hadn't seen her this happy in a while, and even though she'd always kept on her game face — and would till the end — today she was beaming. Certainly no one seeing us that day would have known that our destination was the Memorial Sloan-Kettering Cancer Center.

Like Pop, Mom was the real deal, made of tough stock. Born and raised in Peoria, Illinois, the daughter of John Boyd Stone, chairman of the board of the First National Bank of Peoria, she attended Foxcroft School, then followed her heart to the New York stage, where she met and fell in love with a feisty young actor named Jack Lemmon. The two of them went on to star in four different live television series together (including the very early sitcoms *That Wonderful Guy* and *Heaven for Betsy*), then moved together to Hollywood, where his career took off. And then, in a matter of a few years, she'd seen their marriage crumble away to nothing.

And here she was on this sunny day in New York: sixty-two-year-old, Emmy-nominated actress Cynthia Stone, walking through Central Park with her two little duckies. Only one thing was

123

wrong: she was dying of cancer.

I happened to be with her on the visit to her doctor a year before, when he told her that stat bloodwork had come back with disappointing results. I knew the news had hit her hard, but she did not let slip any indication of fear or shock. She wouldn't do that in front of her child; showing anything less than absolute strength was never an option for her. Actually, the struggle had begun two years earlier, when, during a routine operation, the doctor found that she had colon cancer, and that it already had metastasized to the surrounding organs. Now, two years later, here was Mom heading back to the hospital, ready to fight one last battle, but knowing in her heart that this would probably be the last spring day she'd have to walk through Central Park.

The kind of strength that Mom showed then, and that my father would show fifteen years later, is not easily come by; these were people of a different generation, stronger and more resilient.

Both Mom and Pop had also faced medical problems when they were young, and they never stopped fighting. My mother had been struck by polio as a child, suffering a paralysis of her entire left side for over six months. And Pop, who was often sick as a child, through his youth had annual bouts of mastoiditis (an inflammation of the ear), causing him to endure weeks of pain and almost daily visits from the local doctor who'd tend to the draining of the infection. Pop said the sight of the bespectacled old guy reaching for his ear, and the resultant pain of the procedure, created a reflex action that all his life caused him to pull back whenever anyone reached out to touch his head.

After our walk in the park that afternoon, when the doctor at Sloan-Kettering came into the examining room to meet Mom, a patient who'd been diagnosed as terminal, she found all of us telling jokes and laughing. The doctor, who was one of the best in the world, minus the bedside manner, stared at us like we were nuts, but Mom, with her ever-present dignity, introduced herself and explained our behavior by saying that we'd simply had such a marvelous day.

I remember the doctor pulled me aside and asked if Mom fully understood her situation. I explained that she did — that we all did — but that she was the strongest person any of us would ever know and this was how she would face whatever was ahead of her. And in fact, Mom remained that way to the end, making every arrangement herself, from the largest to the smallest, even going so far as to schedule flights, hotels, and rental cars for her own funeral.

Mom's ultimate display of strength, though, came when she made up her mind that she was going to see one more Christmas. Despite the doctor's dire ultimatum of "September at the latest," she'd done exactly that.

On Christmas Eve, her entire family gathered at her house in Miami, where she'd insisted on being for her final days. As we sat at the dinner table, Bud, her husband, brought her out of the bedroom to tearful applause. She'd cheated the grim reaper by three months, and she'd managed to remain strikingly beautiful through it all.

I remember she looked at each one of us for a long moment — her eyes still alert, still aware — and then she took her husband's hand, smiled one last elegant smile, and went back into the bedroom. She fell asleep that night and never woke again. Two days later she was gone.

Though she was taken from us at a criminally early age, I thank God she was here long enough to meet my bride, Gina. I was a Lemmon, after all, and would need careful looking after. I just wish she could have met her grandchildren.

Mom was laid to rest in Peoria. At her funeral I remember seeing Pop cry, and it struck me at that moment that, though I'd seen him do that very thing numerous times on film, I'd never before seen him cry in real life. Later, I learned that not only had the loss of Mom, and my reaction to it, been deeply moving for him, but that it had allowed him momentarily to turn away from the influence of his stiff New England upbringing and to cry over the loss of his own parents as well — something he previously had not been able to do.

That afternoon, as I walked away from the burial site, the finality of it all hit me, and my knees momentarily weakened. I remember Pop was right there, holding me up and helping me down the path to the waiting car.

And as I looked down at him now, lying in his hospital bed, fighting the same fight my mother had, so valiantly, those many years before, I said a quiet thank you. He'd been there to hold me up many times in my life, but that time — that was a biggie.

Chapter Twelve

PEBBLE BEACH (PART TWO)

"This is the year, Jack! This is the year!"

The chant I'd grown so accustomed to hearing over the last decade echoed out over the hallowed eighteenth green at Pebble Beach. Once again, everything seemed to be happening in slow motion, as it did every time I stepped onto this magnificent green, in this incredible place, during this impossible time.

The chant grew to a roar, and I turned my gaze away from the whitecapped waves of the Pacific Ocean. The gallery, hundreds thick, were on their feet, screaming their approval as Peter Jacobsen, my father's long-standing pro partner in the Pebble Beach Pro-Am and the man who'd figuratively carried my father on his back for the last eleven years, hoisted Pop up once again and physically carried him onto the green. Of course the gallery loved it — that's why they loved Pebble, the stars and their hijinks

The toll of another exhausting week
at Pebble. Once more, not making
the cut, but still game.

— and Pop never disappointed.

Reaching the green, he hopped off Jacobsen's back and did a little two-step for the crowd. They ate it up; their beloved everyman had arrived and was doing a jig on the short grass.

Then, in mid-step, he looked over at me, caught my eye, and smiled that smile of his I'd seen so many times in the past, the one that said, "Hey, kiddo, maybe next year." That's when I took the snapshot; that's when the camera inside my head went *click*.

That photo went into the big album, the one I'm paging through right now, these many years later, the one filled with thousands of pictures, thousands of memories. First up is the picture of Pop and Jake twitching while I played out the final hole of the Celebrity Scramble against Mark McGwire years before. No, Pop hadn't made the cut that year (as we all know), and no, neither had I. In fact, over time I'd actually managed to display such ineptitude on the links that I'd earned quite a reputation for myself as well, one that almost rivaled Pop's.

Following Pebble, Pop and I had played with the pros again at the Bob Hope Classic in Palm Springs, where we added to the Lemmon Legacy by terrorizing unsuspecting galleries and doing untold damage to both the game of golf and the reputable name of Mr. Hope.

We fell off bridges, broke windows, and practically destroyed the delicate desert ecosystem, all the while covering our path with a blanket of apologies. We used to have two-dollar side-bets at all times, and would have to "truthfully" report our scores at the end of each day. I can assure you that virtually none of them was in the two-digit range.

Despite our always less-than-stellar scores, there were individual moments of glory. One of my favorite memories of those days was getting to see Pop occasionally pull off some impossible move, make a stroke that was brilliant, after which he would invariably pump the air with his fist, happiness radiating from every pore, and scream, "Now that's a touch of terrific!"

I did, though, once manage to put together a whole round of good shots, giving me a banner day — one of those times when, as they say, golf pays you back. I'd been paired with Davis Love at Bermuda Run, one of the really great courses in Palm Springs, and evidently the evil god who monitored the Lemmon Legacy wasn't watching that day, because I managed to shoot a 78 on my own ball, one of the best rounds I ever played. And that I did it with Davis Love makes it a day that definitely goes in the big chest of great memories. Pop, of course, was both very proud and extremely jealous.

The following year I was fortunate enough to be invited back to Pebble, where something happened that I will never be able to take back or make amends for, at least as far as Pop was concerned.

I'm ashamed to even acknowledge it, but

since I promised myself when I set out to tell these stories that I would include it all, the good and the bad, I am forced to admit that the following year at Pebble I did something so foul, so odious and under-handed, so despicable and downright awful, that it pains me to acknowledge it: At the 1994 Pebble Beach Pro-Am, while partnered with professional Andy Bean, I made the cut.

Just as I swore then, I swear now: I had nothing to do with it. It was like some out-side force was guiding my hand, enabling me somehow to put together three rounds in the eighties and . . . And . . . And my father will never forgive me, not even for the rest of eternity. Oh sure, he was a good sport about it at the time, even pretended to get all excited, but as good an actor as he was, he couldn't cover the pain of a be-trayal that cut so deep. One Lemmon just did not do this to another.

He did, however, follow me around the course the next day analyzing every move I made and instructing me on every nuance of my game. Remembering Jake's advice during the Celebrity Shootout years be-fore, I listened carefully to every one of Pop's tips, thanked him, then went and did the exact opposite. The result was we took twelfth place, and while Andy Bean was technically my partner in play, the truth is, it was Pop there beside me the whole time, having a ball finally playing magic Sunday.

I couldn't know then that Pop would never ever make the cut, so I can only hope that the excitement we had that Sunday, and the thrill we shared of doing it together, was the next best thing.

The middle years at Pebble, and the other great tournaments like the Hope and the L.A. Open, exist like a mobile collage in my mind. Every once in a while, an image swings into focus, such as one of Jake and Greg Norman screaming, "Fore!" and then hurtling golf balls at a porta-potty they thought Pop was using, only to have an old lady walk out instead, dazed and confused. You see, after his usual pre-pee announcement — "If I'm not back in five minutes, call for the cops!" — Jake and Greg thought they'd seen Pop go inside the porta-potty, but he'd actually ducked around back, to, as he so delicately put it, "shake the dew off the lily" in the great outdoors.

Then there was the time Pop and I were playing the desert and our group dumped our drives into a ditch around which there were a bunch of signs that read BEWARE RATTLESNAKES! We all left our balls in the ditch rather than brave an encounter with the snakes, and at the end of the day, as we were playing the home-hole opposite, we looked over to see a ten-year-old kid walking back to his house with the BEWARE RATTLESNAKES! signs slung over one shoulder and a huge bag of golf balls over the other. I remember Pop barking a laugh, and saying, "There goes a future president!"

But of all the memories from those middle years, the one that stands out most was not a happy one. It happened as we were about to get into the van to head for the airport on yet another missed Big Sunday. I watched as Pop came down the stairs from his room, moving a little more slowly and stiffly than usual.

I noticed, but racked it up to the fact that this was a seventy-year-old guy who'd just endured a physical test that would challenge a Navy Seal. Walking and playing these steep courses in tournament is tough enough when the weather's good, let alone during a big Pacific storm like the one we'd endured that week. But as I walked over to him to give him a hug, I noticed something that rocked me in my shoes: Pop's eyes weren't focusing, and his speech had a slight slur to it.

When I asked him how he was feeling, he gave me his usual, "Hello, operator, bad connection," and when I pressed a little harder, he resorted to his "Go fuck yourself." But it was evident that something was wrong, and after a conversation with the rest of the family, he agreed to go in for an exam.

When nothing was found, I chalked the incident up to fatigue and disappointment, but then three weeks later, while I was driving back to the hotel from the third days' play at the Bob Hope Invitational, I got a phone call telling me that Pop had entered a hospital and had been diagnosed with a stroke.

True to his New England roots, Pop had never given high priority to the health side of his diet, a subject that invariably got the dismissive "Hello, operator" treatment when it was raised — not surprising for someone whose favorite meal was cheeseburgers, fries, and a chocolate shake. But Pop's "Hello, operator" attitude finally had gotten him into trouble; he'd developed obstructions in both his carotid arteries. The condition was deemed safer to live with, however, than to do something about, and Pop, as always, underplayed it beautifully, with lots of "Hello, operator"s and "Go fuck yourself"s. And as always, he kept going, kept striding forward, kept giving great performances, kept loving (and desecrating) golf, and yes, kept sneaking cheeseburgers and shakes on the side.

The following year found him back at Pebble, because come hell or high water (or even a job, for that matter), Jack Lemmon was not going to miss the tournament at Pebble Beach.

And not only did he make it to Pebble Beach the year following his stroke, by the second day of play, it was clear that there was a distinct possibility that this year Jack Lemmon was finally, finally going to make the cut. He was actually going to do it this time, this time for sure.

Pop had been playing lights-out, and Jake was like a house on fire, so there was no way they weren't going to make it. I, on the other hand, was faithfully carrying on the Lemmon Legacy of sitcom golf, actually managing to land one of my shots in a course-side party's punch bowl. But none of that nonsense made any difference, because the big guy, the Human Hinge, was gonna do it this year, and you could feel the electricity everywhere on the course.

Under Dave Pelz's tutelage (Pop somehow

got the great golf guru to caddy for him too), by Friday, Pop was already closing in on the score he would need to make the cut the next afternoon. It was a truly great day, hearing the renewed vigor in that perennial chant, "This is the year, Jack!"

And suddenly it was: This *was* the year, Jack! And let me tell you something — that fact was not lost on Jack either. He was holding high court at Pebble, shuffling, jigging, and throwing one-liners at a rate that astonished even Jake and me.

The man was positively ebullient, playing those final holes with a double-strut, creaming the ball straight down the center, then converting for a shot at birdie. The guy was honestly playing great golf, and if he played like this the next day, hell, forget the cut, he might even win the damn tournament!

But that was not to be.

The following day found pro and celebrity alike, the whole stinkin' tournament, sitting in the tent at the practice field, solemnly nursing their cups of coffee as torrential rainstorms raged outside.

The silence was palpable inside the tent, which was filled to capacity with recognizable faces, all staring off into oblivion. Pop was there too, head in hands, swearing he was cursed. I, of course, knew better — this was no curse, it was simply the Lemmon Legacy (although sometimes they seemed like the same thing).

And then, as if in cosmic agreement, a disgruntled and soaked PGA official marched into the tent and announced, "This tournament is officially called for all amateur and celebrity contestants!"

A sour look still on his face, the official clomped back out. There was a long silence, and then Clint Eastwood said, "So what do we do now?"

Pop played a few more pro-ams at Pebble Beach after that, but every time the cut eluded him. In fact, he even got rained out *again* while playing with our good buddy Andy Garcia one year when I couldn't attend because of work.

The year he'd gotten too sick to play, he and I watched the tournament from his hospital room, rooting for Jake the whole way. Jake didn't win the tournament that last year, but he did make the cut, and as Pop watched him play on magic Sunday, I could tell he was imagining himself out there, walking those fairways, making some impossible shot, pumping his fist into the air one more time and yelling, "Now that's a touch of terrific!"

An early
snapshot of
Pop, already a
fisherman.

Mom and Pop
on their wedding
day, searching
for approval
from Papa Jack.

Newlyweds playing newlyweds on an
early TV sitcom, *Heaven For Betsy*.

Newlyweds at home, with me, posing for a
1955 movie magazine spread.

Pop with me and GG, his mom, during one of his frequent visits to the beach house.

Pop and me on our first fishing trip.

Pop gives me a comforting arm after I was thrown out at second.

Visiting Pop on my favorite of all his movie sets, *The Great Race.*

A visit to another movie set, and I get to meet President Fred Astaire.

Pop and GG and the Lemmon smile, at full blaze.

The Lemmon smile strikes again, this time on me, here with my sister Courtney.

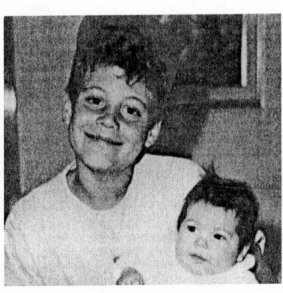

A favorite picture, Pop and me at work together on *That's Life*.

Taking up the game of golf got Pop and me even closer together. Victory at Pebble Beach may have eluded us, but the experience of playing there provided many great memories.

Two happy golfing amateurs and our last gig together.

Pop and Uncle Waltz (Walter Matthau) with Sydney, my daughter, right after the release of *Grumpy Old Men*.

Pop at the Connecticut house, playing with Syd while holding Chris Jr.

The Legacy continues. Three little Lemmons — Sydney, Christopher, and Jonathan — on Pop's favorite holiday, Christmas.

Chapter Thirteen

He'd done it again . . . Pop had beaten back the beast by drawing on one of the positive aspects of the Lemmon Legacy: courage. Just like Papa Jack, who only days before his death had so valiantly waved out the window of the ICU to his young grandson, Pop had drawn on inner strength and had come through a devastating surgery, getting well enough to go home again. Still on heavy doses of chemo, and having to deal with a colostomy, it was anything but easy for him, but he faced it as he had everything else in his life — without complaint and with utter conviction. Exercising daily and even taking meetings for upcoming projects, he remained an optimist to the end.

THE HILLS ARE BURNING

November 6, 1961, saw the worst brush fire to date in the history of Southern Cali-

A cool afternoon.

fornia, the Bel Air fire. One of my most vivid memories from very early childhood was standing with my father in the yard of his home in Beverly Glen Canyon and watching the fire crest the top of the ridge opposite us.

As the fire closed in, we stood there staring, helpless to do anything. I remember that when Pop finally said it was time to go because the flames would soon be at the house, I'd started blowing as hard as I could, a seven-year-old's attempt to blow out the fire.

This charming little one-bedroom home in the hills had been where my father lived for as long as I could remember. It had a wonderful — and to me at that age, magical — garden that I could spend hours in, running from dragons and battling knights. It had an incredible view of the canyon below, allowing me to lob stones at passing trolls and assorted foes. It was a little boy's wonderland, and I was damned if any brush fire was going to burn it up.

I was very young then, so I don't have a lot of memories of those days, but most of those that I do have, and which I treasure, are centered around that little house. Pop would have me there for a sleepover from time to time, and I remember great Hollywood parties during which I would overhear passionate discussions of life, the arts, and romance, arguments that would rage into the night.

I usually would be ensconced in Pop's intimate little study, fighting to stay awake, but with reality gradually blurring to dreams as I fell asleep on the sofa.

But on occasion my youthful curiosity would get the upper hand, and I would wake myself up and, dragging my blanket, wander down the dimly lit hallway to where the action was. Due to Pop's eclectic taste in art, which ranged from pre-Colombian to post-Pollock, my overly active imagination always found this journey daunting, especially since I had to sneak by the statues of two spooky Persian women who I was convinced would come to life and start chasing me. But when I finally arrived at the end of the hall, and lay my blanket on the floor, my head positioned so that I could peek around the corner, the reward was always worth the journey.

Pop loved telling the story about the famous writer Dorothy Parker, who, after the late-night post-wedding party following her second marriage (to writer Alan Campbell), fell back against the wall, gazed at her new husband, and said, "Ahhh, alone at last . . . Except for you."

That was exactly how I would feel on those magical/scary nights, with the Persian statues held safely at bay by the glow of the party I was eavesdropping on. In the room were all the familiar faces I'd seen countless times, not just in my father's home, but also on television and at the movies, all so animated and full of life. And there would be Pop, at the piano, surrounded by friends, creating that magic that lit up the room.

Alone at last . . . Except for all of you.

The year before the great Bel Air fire,

Pop had taken me on our first adventure: to fire off model rockets in the desert. I loved building those rockets, and Pop decided to take me out to what was then wilderness to launch them. We stayed at a little motel that was situated next door to a trout farm. The fish farm had two big cement lakes filled with rainbow trout, and to a six-year-old kid, this was a great and wondrous thing.

Sunrise on the following morning found me raring to go, but Pop was still sound asleep. Not wanting to get our adventure off on the wrong foot, I pondered the best possible way to wake Pop, and eventually arrived at the brilliant notion of getting someone else to do it. I quietly called the man who ran the little motel and ordered what I thought would be Pop's favorite thing for breakfast. A half-hour later, the old guy showed up at the door with a triple martini.

Whether Pop appreciated being awakened in that manner, I don't remember, but I do recall that we had a banner day, shooting off rockets and climbing through the San Gabriel Mountains, in search of mischief. And then, before sundown, we arrived back at the trout farm, where Pop set me up with a rod and some bait, and then —

having heard about a hot poker game back at the motel — left me to do my thing.

Pop's luck must've been with him that afternoon, because it was dark out when he finally returned to find me sitting on a mountain of trout. Hopefully whatever he won at poker was enough to cover the cost of all those fish I'd caught.

Of course, looking back now as a father myself, the fact that Pop had left me alone like that does raise a few questions. Granted, those were more innocent times, but were Pop's actions inadvertently irresponsible, or have we as a society grown overly protective, not allowing our kids enough freedom to find their own way? Difficult to say. As a kid, I remember waking before the sun and running Santa Monica beach with my beloved dog, Ensign Pulver, just the two of us. It's something I could never let my children do now.

But there is one thing I can say with absolute honesty and assurance: There was never a time when I was with Pop that I didn't feel loved and secure — and, most important, there was no time that I didn't feel the magic.

Fortunately, the great fire didn't get Pop's house after all, having stopped short on the opposite hillside, right where I'd blown it out. There were other forces at work, though, and too soon that house and the magic I'd known there would be a part of my young past.

One day not long after the fire, Pop brought me up to the house, saying there was someone important he wanted me to meet. When we pulled into the driveway, the front door of the little house opened and a woman came out. She smiled at me.

Pop put his arm around her, and he smiled too. Then she said, "Hello, Christopher, my name is Felicia: I'm your father's new wife."

I smiled back and then she laughed; I remember her laugh was powerful and a bit frightening. She laughed and said, "I'm the wicked stepmother."

Soon after that I had to say good-bye to the magic world of Beverly Glen. Pop moved with Felicia and her daughter, Denise, to a house the next canyon over, and a few years later, when my sister Courtney arrived, his new life was complete.

Complete except for one very important thing: five years after the great Bel Air fire, someone else would enter Pop's life as well, someone who would change it completely.

Chapter Fourteen

We spoke with Pop's doctors, nice guys, genuinely nice guys, but it's hard to think of them that way when they're handing out bad news. Only weeks before, Pop had braved a really tough time and had come back, able once again to go home and sleep in his own bed.

Gina and I had flown out with the kids for Easter and found him looking great. Overnight, however, all that changed. The worst possible enemy had struck — pneumonia. With cancer it's usually not the disease that kills in the end, but rather the secondary infections that take advantage of a weakened immune system, and more times than not, that means pneumonia.

Pop was on a ventilator now, heavily medicated and sleeping. When he did awaken, it usually meant the breathing tube had to be purged, drawn up out of his chest, which made him cough and gag uncontrollably.

That process usually would take pretty much all of his energy, and afterward he would fall asleep again, exhausted.

This time there seemed little point to staying in his room with him. He would rarely wake, and when he did he would barely regain consciousness. And until the pneumonia was overcome, that situation would not change.

But still I stayed, watching, remembering . . .

MAGIC TIME

Aside from "Son, there's lots of assholes out there," two other of my father's aphorisms I remember best both pertained to acting. One was "Simple is best," and the other was widely known in the business as Dad's trademark. As far as any of us know, it was something he said before every take, on every film he ever made.

I was visiting him on the set of *The Front Page* one day back in 1973 when I heard him say it for at least the hundredth time. He closed his eyes, effortlessly slipping into the character of Hildy Johnson, then he said, "Magic time . . . ," and walked onto the set, once again to stand toe-to-toe with the man and the actor who had become and would remain so significant a part of his life, both on-screen and off.

When Walter Matthau entered Pop's world, he became more than just his best friend; Walter was like the brother Pop never had. *The Front Page* was their third film together, eight years after legendary director Billy Wilder had teamed them originally in the dark comedy *The Fortune Cookie*. A strong bond of friendship had formed between them from the outset, and it would endure the rest of their lives.

My in-laws, Pat and Dan Raymond, tell the story of leaving Walter's house one night after a get-together and looking back to see six-foot-four Walter planting a kiss on five-foot-eight Pop's forehead. They said the sight was at once farcical and touching.

Pop and Walter made ten films together, although *The Fortune Cookie* got them off to a very unpromising — and slightly scary — start when Walter suffered a heart attack shortly before production commenced. That Pop and Walter developed an immediate friendship and trust is evidenced by a story my father used to tell about those first days.

While still recovering in the hospital,

Walter (who, as legend has it, enjoyed placing a wager from time to time) handed Pop an envelope, asking him to make a payoff to his bookie.

"Just meet him outside Fox Studios at three, Lemmon," Walter had crooned. "You're a pal."

Pop dutifully showed up at the appointed hour and encountered a three-hundred-pound guy with cauliflower ears, a mushroom nose, and a heavy drawl. He ripped open the envelope, thumbed a batch of hundreds, smiled, then looked down at my father and said, "Tanks, Mistah Lemmon! Ya know youz my faverite actuh. Howz about a autograph!" So there was Pop, giving an autograph to Walter Matthau's bookie in front of Fox Studios.

Pop wasn't the only Lemmon to have a venture-staked run-in with Waltz; I became a proud member of that club as well. One year, at Pop's annual Christmas party, I was recounting to a friend the tale of a recent streak of blind luck I'd had at the track. I'm not a gambler, but I'm also not averse to throwing a few twenties on the table. At the time I knew a guy who was a really talented artist, but like many artists found it difficult to support his creative process, so on the side he was a really talented handicapper. After he told me about a streak of good fortune he'd had at the track, I took the plunge on a hunch, handed him fifty bucks, told him to throw it on his next pony's nose, and keep it riding. My friend did, and through some crazy fluke, I ended up winning four times in a row.

It was while I was telling that story at the party that I heard Walter's unmistakable voice chime up from behind me.

"*Excuuuse* me, Lemmon? Did I just hear you correctly? Four ponies in a row at seven to one?"

"Hi, Waltz. Yeah. Crazy, isn't it? I don't know what the exact odds were, but it was something like that."

"And I've got a Martian living in my house," he said with his perfect deadpan.

"Waltz, I'm not making it up, it did happen."

"His name's Harry, and he's from Mars."

"I tell you what, the next time my buddy calls with a tip I'll let you know about it. Okay?" I offered.

"Harry and I'll be waiting," Walter replied, and he was gone.

A couple of weeks later I got a call from my buddy. He had a five-to-one shot running at Hollywood Park the next afternoon that he felt good about.

"Really good, Billy?" I asked. "I mean, we're talkin' Uncle Waltz here."

"Really good," Billy replied. So I went ahead and made the call.

Walter's classic drawl came back at me over the phone: "This is NASA speaking."

"Okay, Waltz, I got your winner right here. Horse number five in the third race. Her name's Kylie's Pride."

"Kylie's Pride. Won't put more than two hundred on her so I don't change the odds. And your buddy feels good about this one, eh, Lemmon?"

"A sure winner," I shot back, more surely than I actually felt.

The next day at just about lunchtime the bell went off for the third race at Hollywood Park. There were seven horses in the starting gate, but only six of them made it out.

Horse number five, an insufferable nag named Kylie's Pride, fell down. Just fell down, right there in the starting gate. It was like someone had pulled a string and all four legs went out from underneath her. The jockey was left sitting in the saddle, two feet off the ground. Finally he just got up and walked off the track. Kylie's Pride got up too, and slowly followed him off. It was the worst performance ever executed by a horse in the history of Hollywood Park.

Needless to say I didn't call Uncle Waltz back right away after that. But a couple of days later, I came home to a message on my machine.

"Lemmon?" The voice poured out like liquid. "This is your uncle Walter."

I dropped my head into my hands.

"You know that Martian I was telling you about, the one living in my house?"

"Oh boy," I said to the empty room.

"Well his relatives moved in."

Shortly after Pop's clandestine meeting in front of Fox, Walter recovered from his heart attack, and filming on *The Fortune Cookie* commenced. The film went on to be a success, leading to Pop and Walter's next film, *The Odd Couple*, which would cement the team's place in cinematic history.

In addition to respecting him greatly as an actor, Pop loved Walter's sense of humor, which would manifest itself at the most unpredictable times. During the filming of *Buddy Buddy*, Walter took a perilous fall off a scaffolding while doing a stunt. It turned out that he wasn't seriously injured, but that wasn't immediately apparent, and he was, indeed, badly shaken.

Pop, beside himself with concern, thought this was the end for his good buddy. He folded up his jacket and placed it under Walter's head. Then, holding Waltz in his arms, and with tears in his eyes, he looked down and asked, "Are you comfortable?" To which Walter replied, "I make a living." Pop adored Walter, and cantankerous Waltz adored him right back.

Except for *Buddy Buddy*, Billy Wilder's swan song, and a film that got a decidedly lukewarm reception from both the critics and the public, almost twenty years would pass between *The Front Page* and Pop and Walter's next movie. But they more than made up for it in 1993 when the duo of Lemmon and Matthau came back big with the out-of-left-field smash hit *Grumpy Old Men*. I remember seeing Pop after the success of *Grumpy*, and I sensed immediately that it seemed like a huge weight had been lifted off his shoulders. Not only had this movie put him and Walter back on the map, it was the first big commercial hit for Pop in a while as well, and in a profession as perilous as acting, where there are no guarantees (except, of course, that you'll probably fail), this was a blessed event, one that allowed Pop to sit back and relax a little.

It was about time.

Unfortunately, the closeness that existed between these two men was dealt a tough blow during the filming of *Grumpy Old Men 2*. The problem actually arose not between Pop and Waltz, but between Felicia and Waltz's wife, Carol, and such sway did the wives have over their husbands that the friendship was severely tested. What had been an inseparable foursome, overnight — for what appeared to be the silliest of reasons — was disbanded.

Yet Pop and Walter went on to make two more films together — *Out to Sea* and *The Odd Couple II* — and despite the tidal pull to distance them (a phenomenon I knew only too well), they stayed best friends to the end, their bond of friendship one of the all-time great show-business buddy relationships. In fact, if only Walter had learned to play golf, I think Pop would have married him.

Chapter Fifteen

LAST OF THE SHTARKERS

When professional golfers hear the term "country club," they probably think of places with names like St. Andrews, Shinnecock Hills, or Augusta National. But there are thousands of less exalted country clubs scattered across the nation, little gems that have become a way of life for many, many people. Each of these clubs has its own identity, its own personality, its own history; and each becomes a small world in itself, where strangers meet and become lifelong friends, and where they spend some of the most prized and cherished times of their lives. And because of that, pretty much every club is going to have great stories — tales and anecdotes their members hand down from generation to generation, embellishing and enlarging them with each retelling.

Like any place else, Los Angeles has its fair share of great country clubs, Riviera, home of the L.A. Open, and Sherwood Country Club being prime examples. But at the heart of the city lie a number of clubs with less exalted names, little gems like Bel Air, Lakeside, and Hillcrest, clubs that, though they may not be world famous, are very special in their own right, because they traditionally have been at the heart of old Hollywood.

These are the clubs at which W. C. Fields would tee off, or Esther Williams would take an afternoon swim; where Bob Hope and Bing Crosby would go head-to-head on the eighteenth, taking no prisoners. These were the country clubs of the stars, and the stories that came out of these venerable institutions are on a whole different level than those from any others on earth.

My father had the great pleasure of being invited to join Hillcrest Country Club. Although the membership at Hillcrest was predominately Jewish, and Pop was Catholic, there were no restrictions to keep him from joining, and since Hillcrest is truly a gem of a country club and has a very personable membership, Pop was delighted by their offer and immediately accepted — and, of course, as a part of that package, came an equally delighted me.

We spent many great years there, playing unforgettable rounds of golf with some of our best buddies, many of them also actors, like Andy Garcia, Sidney Poitier, and Dennis Quaid, and out of these rounds came some great stories.

I remember once when I slammed a drive out-of-bounds and started throwing a tantrum, Joey Pesce advised me to calm down because the only golfers who deserved to get upset when they hit a bad shot were the pros, because the pros were the only ones who could truly play the game. And then, without missing a beat, he hit an enormous shanker himself and screamed every four-letter word known to mankind.

I remember my father once hit two back-to-back shots so badly that the first one smacked a passing car, causing it to stop and then the second one broke the car's windshield.

And there was the time right after a freak L.A. hailstorm that I encountered Sidney Poitier on the fifth hole, his cart careening down the middle of the fairway doing three-sixties while Sidney held on for dear life, yelling, "This is not funny! This is not funny!"

Pop loved the hours spent on the golf

course — despite his shortcomings on the tee, and the fairways, *and* the green. He never tired of playing the game, and fortunately, he never lost his sense of humor about golf.

In fact, some of his most treasured stories were prized anecdotes created by master storytellers and handed down from one golfing generation to the next. And the stories that abounded at Hillcrest were second to none.

Hillcrest had its own "Round Table," but it was not Arthur's knights who sat there. This table was home to the "Shtarkers" (a Yiddish term; loosely translated, "big shots"), the men who invented funny. It was their humor that had created vaudeville, and helped to build Hollywood. Among these greats were the likes of Milton Berle, the Marx Brothers, Jack Benny, and Danny Thomas. And the king of this Round Table was the greatest of them all, Mr. George Burns.

For his ninety-fifth birthday, Hillcrest threw George Burns a roast. It was a big event and Pop and I were invited to perform. Honored, we accepted the invitation and put together a little number to sing for George, utilizing two pianos. On the night of the roast we showed up about an hour before showtime, went onstage, did a sound check, and then were invited to wait backstage. We headed to the executive offices of the club that were serving as the backstage area, opened the doors, looked in, and our jaws dropped. Sitting in the room were pretty much all the surviving members of the Round Table, with George, the king, holding court.

Pop and I must have made an odd sight, standing in the doorway, our mouths agape, because everyone stopped talking and turned and stared right back at us. There was a long silence, then Burns said, "Hey look, a coupl'a Lemmons."

Pop and I remained speechless for the next hour (yes, that is possible) as each one of the Shtarkers told stories about the hidden secrets of Hillcrest CC. These stories were so plentiful that George Burns actually had to time each teller by checking his wristwatch and calling out, "Ten seconds, five seconds, time! Sammy, you're up!"

By the time Pop and I had found a seat, comic Jan Murray was just finishing up the story of the famous tallywhacker duel between Milton Berle (reported by his fellow Shtarkers to be of monstrous proportions) and Lakeside Country Club's pride and joy, Forest Tucker. Reportedly both men laid it on the table, so to speak, in the men's locker room, and to the greater glory of Hillcrest, Uncle Miltie won by a nose — or would that be a head?

"Ten seconds, five seconds, time!" Burns called. The room was electric with energy. "Miltie, you couldn't ask for a better intro than that."

Berle ceased bowing to the applause and took the stage as only he could, then launched into the story of Chico Marx and the Eucalooka tree, a tale that became a favorite for my father.

All four Marx brothers were beloved members of Hillcrest and spent a great deal of time there, but of the four it was Chico who had the deepest passion for golf. He loved to play the game and he loved to bet on the game — and from what I've heard, it's fortunate he made a good living.

Chico had a regular group he would play with once or twice a week, and the money would fly. Chico also had what golfers call an "angry duck hook," which meant that he'd slam the ball way out to the right, and then, in midair, it would veer violently back, turning left, toward its original target. Hitting a draw from right to left can be a good thing if it's done in a controlled manner, but evidently Chico's hook was so heinous that people on neighboring fairways were known to take cover when he was in the neighborhood.

Now, according to the story, it just so happened that there was a huge eucalyptus tree two hundred yards out on the eleventh fairway, right where someone who has an "angry duck hook" would have to aim. Knowing this (and knowing as well Chico's propensity to take on just about any challenge), his fellow players would raise the stakes to astronomic heights whenever they reached the eleventh hole. And invariably, Chico's drive would curve straight into the trunk of that damn eucalyptus tree. And invariably, he'd jump up and down, screaming, "Goddamn Eucalooka tree" (unfortunately, watching Milton Berle jump up and down while imitating Chico Marx's thick Brooklyn accent can't be described in words). "I'm comin' out here wit a axe, I'm tellin' ya I'm gonna chop dat bastard down!" And still the game continued.

Over the years the bets increased, along with Chico's frustration, and finally one day Chico had enough. Standing on the eleventh tee, a cold sweat dripping from his brow, he took his swing and watched as his ball traced its inevitable arc toward *Eucalyptus globulus N.O. Myrtaceae.*

"Sonofabitch-bastards!! That's it!!" he screamed. Then he turned to his playing partners who were doing their best to control their laughter.

"You tink dis is funny, huh? Every time dat goddamn Eucalooka tree gets me, huh? Pretty funny, huh?" At that his partners fell out, enraging Chico all the further.

"All right, I'm tellin' you what. Next week, I'm bettin' youz ten tousand dollars, longest drive, right 'ere!"

Despite their protests, Chico persisted, and the bet was on. It was all the talk of the club, and as the week wore on, furious side betting was observed from the course to the card room. It got to the point where daily odds were being displayed in the pro shop. As the day of reckoning grew closer, the tension in the air was almost palpable.

Chico was seen on the practice range, a place he'd barely acknowledged in the past, furiously hitting drive after drive, and taking as many lessons as humanly possible with the club pro — all to no avail. The "angry duck hook" only got worse. In fact, it got to the point where Chico's only hope of hitting the range in front of him

170

was to aim pretty much perpendicular to it, directly at the clubhouse, which reportedly got the attention of more than one luncheon group seated on the veranda.

Finally, when the morning of the competition arrived, Chico's playing partners found themselves waiting on the first tee with a sizeable gallery of senior club members gathered to watch the match. Fifteen minutes after their start time had been called, there still was no sign of Chico, and the members were starting to murmur about a no-show. But then, cool as a cucumber, he came striding out of the clubhouse, eyeing the crowd of elder members.

"What da hell's goin' on 'round 'ere? Aren't youz guys supposed ta be in da clubhouse playin' cards and dyin'?"

He approached his partners and tipped his hat. "Moinin' boys, shall we's get to it?"

And the game was on. As they played the front nine, the crowd thickened, and at the turn there were close to a hundred people following the group. All noticed how cool Chico seemed compared to his manic state during the previous week. Even his partners noticed the nonchalant attitude he affected through the front nine, as well as the better-than-usual play that accompanied it.

At last Chico and his entourage arrived at the eleventh tee. From the elevated hillock he took a long look out at the hole, then turned and smiled at the throng and his approaching partners.

"Everybody ready for showtime?" he called as the group crested the rise where they could look out over the eleventh fairway.

And there they were greeted by an amazing sight: the "Eucalooka" tree was gone. Chico had hired a bunch of guys to come in during the night and chop it down. There was stunned silence while Chico stood on the tee, chuckling at his playing partners.

"Goddamn Eucalooka tree got what was comin' to it!" he announced. Then he turned, spiked his ball into the ground, aimed totally perpendicular to the fairway, let loose a huge swing, and, for the first time in his natural life, didn't hit an "angry duck hook."

As a matter of fact, he actually slammed the ball straight over the fence of Hillcrest's property line, straight over Motor Avenue and over the fence of Rancho Park golf course across the street, onto the fourteenth green, and straight into MGM boss Louis B. Mayer's rear end.

Later on, in his cups, Chico was heard to lament: "Goddamn Eucalooka tree — now I ain't never woikin' again."

"Time," Burns called as Berle finished his story, and over the howls of laughter the gauntlet was thrown down for the next Shtarker. From then on it was a blur of stories, most of them about dearly departed Knight of the Round Table Jack Benny.

Then the door swung open, and the room was told that it was "showtime," although for Pop and me, the real showtime was over. It would be virtually impossible to top what we'd already experienced.

The whole evening went great. Pop and I had a ball singing and taking verbal jabs at George. Some truly great performers added their magic, and at the end of it all came one last treat.

The room had emptied and the Knights had adjourned to the Round Table itself for a goodnight cigar. To see just six or seven of them sitting around that huge table brought thoughts of what the old days must have been like, when the table was jammed with the full order of Knights, yelling, "Ten seconds, five seconds, time!

Groucho, you're up!"

George Burns was puffing on a cigar bigger than his own head when Danny Thomas called out, "Did ya hear the new club rule, George? Startin' next week, no cigars inside anymore. Looks like the gals got their way."

Burns looked over at him, "Yeah, things change."

A murmur of agreement from the table followed, then Danny smiled at a recollection: "I remember when I first joined this joint. I had a friend who was a member here, and I told him, 'Larry, I'm dyin' ta get into Hillcrest. Somebody told me they let in goyim, is it true?' [Danny, being Lebanese and Catholic, used the term *goyim*, the Yiddish word for a gentile, to describe himself.] 'Of course, it's true!' my buddy told me, and he put me up for membership.

"Coupl'a months goes by, I hear nothin' from Larry, I give him a call: 'Larry, what the hell's goin' on? I thought you told me they took goys at Hillcrest!' Larry shoots back: 'They take goys, Danny, just be patient!'

"A year goes by, I'm callin' this guy every month: 'Larry what's the holdup? You told me they take goys! You told me they take goys!'

"Finally Larry calls back, screaming: 'Will you stop botherin' me, Thomas. I talked to the board! They take goys! But they need to think about it with you, 'cause when they take goys, they want 'em to *look* like goys!' "

A round of chuckles came from those assembled, then Burns stood up.

"Thanks for the party, boys, it was a peach."

There were goodnights all around, and the Round Table was adjourned.

Two weeks later, Danny Thomas, beloved by his fans, his family, and his fellow Knights, passed away in his sleep. Then a few years later it was Uncle Miltie, Mr. TV, who passed as well.

One by one, the Knights fell. The last one, Mr. George Burns, lived to see his hundredth birthday, and then, five years after that night at Hillcrest CC, the King of the Round Table went to join his cohorts, and the last of the Shtarkers was gone.

Though we were never part of that elite group, Pop and I treasured our association with those remarkable men, and continued to repeat their stories to our friends. Over time, they became a part of Pop's legacy, as I hope they will be mine.

Chapter Sixteen

Pop, though still unconscious and on the respirator, was finally showing some sign of improvement. Upon hearing that bit of good news, I left for the East Coast to take care of family and business, having been promised that I'd be notified the second he started coming around. A week later, hearing he'd regained consciousness, I immediately called him.

It was great to hear his voice again. He sounded tired, but still ever optimistic. However, after a few minutes of conversation, I realized he hadn't known I'd been out there with him through those many weeks he'd been unconscious. I remember feeling hurt that no one had told him, but chalked it up to an oversight due to the overwhelming grief we all were experiencing. Of course, none of that made any difference now — Pop had come around and I was going to get the chance to be with him again, and that was all that mattered.

BATTLING THE DRAGON

Days of Wine and Roses was definitely a landmark film in my father's remarkable career, but as will happen with great performances, in many ways, it also defined his life. There was a part of Pop that fit seamlessly with Joe Clay, the character he played in that movie, and that's because a part of him *was* Joe Clay. Walter Matthau, in Joe Baltake's book *The Films of Jack Lemmon*, spoke of Pop as "a good fellow of splendid instincts and deeds," but Walter also spoke of him as a guy who liked to "simmer down to satisfaction from a good cigar and mellow glass of wine."

There was a good reason GG wanted her ashes placed in that urn on the bar at the Ritz Carlton Hotel in Boston, and the reason is that she really liked that place, liked being there, liked drinking there. Put politely, we Lemmons aren't afraid to party, a trait that runs through our family history, and a trait that ran strong in my father. Pop loved, as he called it, "a dram of the elixir of pine-tar and nicotine," and he liked it more than just occasionally. Over the years Pop's partying had gotten a little out of control, had, in fact, gotten to the point where he needed to do something about it.

So he did exactly what everyone would expect Jack Lemmon to do: he kicked the habit, got the monkey off his back, and as with most things he'd done throughout his life, he did it with class.

My father and his second wife, Felicia Farr, had a strong but often volatile relationship. As a matter of fact, their frequent — and public — fights were quite notorious. Whether it was glasses of champagne in the face at an awards benefit or a high-pitched screaming match at Sardi's, they seemed to go at these fights with great abandon, even enjoyment. And as with the drinking, for Pop the public brawling was a way to take a break from his stiff, New England ways and let it all hang out. And for Felicia, it was just who she was — a woman described by a chuckling Billy Wilder as someone who would give you "a knee in the testicles."

In Felicia, Pop found a sparring partner who allowed him to tap into and to explore an emotional arena that previously had been kept under wraps. He found this new freedom viscerally intriguing and indulged in it often. Mr. Wilder also described Pop and Felicia as being members of "the-fight-of-the-week club," which was very true. Pop and Felicia's fights were frequent, furious, and sometimes — although definitely not always — amusing to their Hollywood friends.

Like all excessive behavior, though, these battles took their toll, and eventually had to end. Change finally came in the aftermath of one of their bigger blowouts. Evidently Pop and Felicia had been partying hard the night before, and had gotten into a doozy of a fight. These alcohol-fueled exchanges had grown from alarming but amusing to just plain dangerous, and finally that evening it had gotten serious. An airborne glass ashtray had sliced Pop's forehead, and then smashed through the inch-thick plate-glass window behind him. Betty, the lifelong and beloved housekeeper, had seen enough, and a call had gone out to us three kids.

Though Felicia chose to remain upstairs, Pop had come down to face the music, an ungainly bandage stuck to his head. Apparently he, too, found this a sobering event. He told us with his customary dignity that he'd already been on the phone with the good people at Alcoholics Anonymous, and would be paying them a personal visit shortly.

This decision couldn't have been an easy one for him to make, as it went against so much that he had inherited genetically, and had absorbed socially. Obviously, something aside from a flying ashtray had finally gotten to him. The changes were immediate and radical. Alcohol and cigarettes were out of his life forever, leaving cheeseburgers and chocolate shakes alone to turn to for solace.

Joining AA was a brave decision for Pop, and one that he openly and publicly admitted to and spoke about. It was an action that took astounding guts and was yet another example of his enormous emotional generosity. We kids were all relieved. There had been a few too many events like the one that final evening, and they'd been happening more and more frequently.

One incident in particular that stuck with me through the years. I'm not sure why this one registered so strongly — it wasn't a big deal in the scheme of things — but it stuck, perhaps because its effects went deep. The actual event, though small, also represented a change in my relationship with my father, a change that indicated another force had come into our lives — one that was slowly pushing us apart.

At sixteen years of age, I'd gotten a humdinger of a speeding ticket while driving Pop's car. I was already on shaky ground in the Lemmon household, due to the son-of-the-first-marriage syndrome, and announcement of the ticket generated instant in-house chatter that was, shall we say, not entirely beneficial to my already precarious standing.

Slowly, but ever so surely, I was being edged closer to the door in that house, and once outside, I knew the welcome mat would be withdrawn. I didn't blame my father for this change; it was just something that came with the second marriage, and it wasn't only me for whom the exit door was standing open — anyone who didn't fit with the new agenda, who was, like me, viewed as competition, was shown the way out.

Back in the Lemmon household on that afternoon of the ticket, my name had, in pretty short order, become mud. And having, thanks to previous experience, grown into a shrewd survivalist, by that evening I'd surmised that, at least for the immediate time, away from the house was probably the best place I could possibly be. But as I tried to sneak out, I had had to pass near a small dinner party Felicia was throwing, and I'd been spotted. Evidently there must have been talk about my recent indiscretion, a story told over plentiful amounts of really good Bordeaux. As I passed the dining room, discussion immediately ceased and I found a number of raised brows and slightly judgmental eyes directed at me.

There was a moment of silence, then Pop said, "Oh look, it's the asshole." There was a big laugh, and I was smart enough to recognize an exit line when I heard one.

I spent that night in the comfort of my frequent companion throughout my youth, the beach, where I woke sandy but still whole the next morning.

The "asshole" remark wasn't a big deal on the surface, but underneath that surface there were deep waters. The hurt wasn't purposeful, but it stuck with me, I guess to this day. So when Pop smiled at me that morning fifteen years later, the haphazard bandage hanging off the side of his head, and told me he'd decided to say good-bye to old friends, I couldn't have been more proud of him. He'd made the decision to battle the dragon, a battle he'd fight day by day for the rest of his life. In the process, he also put to rest a part of his personality that had gotten a little severe, a little un-Lemmon-like.

Fortunately, in my life, and as my choice, the tales from the dark side are far outnumbered by those recounting the wonderful times I had with my best friend and father. And seeing the strength he exhibited that day, the day he decided to go it straight and sober, despite the fact that he was doing so alone, is an example of his dignity and class, and that's one thing I'll always remember.

Chapter Seventeen

A DIFFERENT CAREER

My years at California Institute of the Arts were some of the best of my life, a last stab at unbridled innocence. The whole immensity-of-life-and-responsibility thing was still just around the corner. Those years, the fabled 1970s, were truly L.A.'s heyday, and the shiny new school Walt Disney built on a hill in a tiny but growing suburb called Valencia was the talk of the town.

Pop and I were still close, but the distance I'd begun to feel growing between us years earlier, the feeling we were being moved away from each other, was always present. Despite that, our wonderful sojourns in Alaska continued and, more important, music — our favorite means of communication, our bond — remained a steadfast link. It was music that held us together through times that were not always pleasant, music that was an enormous source of joy even during those times that were less than salubrious, and it was music that led my father and me to Cal Arts, where one afternoon we found ourselves shaking hands with the dean of the piano department, the great and terrible wizard of the eighty-eights, Leonid Hambro.

In a very short time I was basically living *Flashdance*, cohabitating with a bunch of other students in a beat-up old house just off campus, where, between us, we were usually able to make the rent and still scrounge up enough money to cook some godawful meals. In other words, we were young, playing at being independent, and it was a great time to be alive.

Pop had just finished filming *The Out-of-Towners*, which proved to be a smash hit for him, and had begun doing some of the more explorative work of his career with films like *Kotch*, *The War Between Men and Women*, *Avanti!*, and, eventually, *Save the Tiger*, the film that would earn him his second Academy Award. During this time we didn't see much of each other, but when we were together, it was always great. Pop loved Cal Arts, loved the artistic honesty and energy of this extraordinary school, and he loved to come visit with me and all my housemates on Walnut Street. The music would start and we would jam for hours.

Cal Arts was a remarkable school, filled with highly motivated students and brilliant mentors and instructors, and it was one of the great gifts of my life to be there.

I studied in three departments: music (my major), theater arts, and dance. Music, though, remained my first love. My big life-plan from as far back as I can remember, jamming with Pop in the Ocean Room of the old Harold Lloyd house, had been to become a world-famous concert pianist. I dreamed of touring Europe playing the Rach III and other impossibly difficult and incredibly romantic works. I dreamed of applause and adulation, but, truth be told, deep down inside I feared I didn't have the chops for it; as it turns out, I was right. I'd paid my musical dues from age five, but I hadn't paid them correctly, a victim of improper study habits and a residence on Santa Monica beach, with all its enticing pastimes. Fortunately I'd been hedging my bets over at the theater department, a pursuit that had always seemed to come more naturally, thanks probably to some of the Lemmon genes passed along by Pop.

When it came time for me to graduate, though, the realization that I now had to go out and actually do something with all this training (like maybe try to make a living) landed on me like a ton of bricks. Haunting me also was the fact that I'd already started landing paying gigs as an actor, yet remained woefully underdeveloped as a "classical" pianist, and music was a dream I was still having trouble letting go.

Just before graduation, however, my musical fantasy received the kiss of death. With no warning, and with only hours to go, Maestro Hambro assigned me to play the three Gershwin Preludes at a joint recital, which also involved five dancers — an assignment another music student had spent weeks preparing for and was very excited to perform — until he came down with double-pneumonia, leaving his colleagues in the dance department with no accompanist.

I frantically practiced the pieces, all too aware that way too soon I'd be in the midst of the first of three live performances, with five dancers, in front of some four hundred people. Unfortunately, Pop wasn't able to make it to any of the performances, something that depressed me a little initially. As things turned out, it was a blessing.

Showtime found me walking onstage in front of a packed house, dressed nattily à la George Gershwin, approaching an old

Baldwin grand, sitting, raising the lid to the keyboard as the lights came up on the five dancers behind me, and launching into the first of Mr. Gershwin's most formidable Preludes.

I made it through the first one okay; I made it through the second (that one is pretty easy), and I'll be damned if I didn't almost make it through the third (which is a beast). Eight bars from the end of the third, the *Prelude in E Flat Minor*, however, I went up (show biz parlance for "blew it," "forgot where I was," and all the other things that happen when your mind suddenly goes blank), high as an eagle — but unfortunately I did it without an eagle's grace.

Now, when you go up as an actor, you can always BS your way out of it, but when you go up playing a piece of solo classical piano music in front of a few hundred people, leaving five dancers onstage in mid-arabesque . . . My friend, you are spanked.

I blew it that night. And then I blew it the next night. Then came the third and final night — my last chance to redeem myself — and damn if I didn't blow it again, on exactly the same note. Three for three. The small show had actually become

188

the hottest ticket on campus solely because everybody wanted to see whether Lemmon would screw the pooch again.

Afterward, as I sat trying to drown my sorrow at Tips Lounge (looking not unlike my father in *The Apartment*), Corey Carson, Johnny's son, a good friend, a good guy, and a good guitarist, came over and plunked down next to me.

"Hey, Lem. Saw the show, man. Guess pretty much everybody on campus has by now."

A look from me, a long pause, then, "Can I give you a piece of advice, as a buddy who cares about you?"

"Yeah. Sure," I said.

"Have you thought about a different career?"

So there it was. After almost two decades of trying, my dream of being a twentieth-century Franz Liszt, of touring the concert halls of Europe, was over. Kaput. Blown away like so much dust off the cover of a baby grand.

Pop lost it when he heard the story. He turned purple, he laughed so hard, then he recounted numerous stories of his own memory lapses and fainting spells, which was sweet of him, but I'm not sure how many of them were true and how much was "Lilac" in origin.

Either way I was off in a new direction, perhaps one that was inevitable: the son of an actor becoming an actor. I took whatever job I could get, working stage, doing showcases, waiting tables, and selling lightbulbs over the phone to support myself. At the same time I continued my studies with my father and mother's teacher from the Actors Studio, the great David Alexander, and augmented those studies with the all-time great comedy-muscles-building improvisation class at Harvey Lembeck's Comedy Workshop, where I'd get the opportunity to spar with the likes of Robin Williams and John Larroquette.

During my studies and in the years that followed, I had good fortune in the business, working almost constantly, which was a blessing. But despite my ability to make a living, my one regret as an actor was that I never got that one perfect role, the one shot at the performance of a lifetime — something I would have loved for my father to have seen.

The play *Love Letters* is a great experience for any actor, though it consists simply of two people sitting on stage reading love letters to each other. It is brilliantly written, and allows the performers to immerse themselves in rich and deeply complex characters as they grow from seventeen to seventy. In the early nineties, Stephanie Zimbalist and I performed the show at the Canon Theater in Beverly Hills, and though we were a little young for the parts, it clicked for us and we enjoyed a successful run.

On closing night, Pop was in the audience for what turned out to be our best performance, and as Steph and I finished, took each other's hand, and turned to the audience for our bow, the full house rose for a standing ovation, and right there in the front row was my father, applauding, whistling, and wiping away a tear. To have gotten that honor from him that night goes high on the list of my greatest moments in life. Very high.

The work continued to come my way, I started to mature as a person, marrying a wonderful woman and starting a family, and Pop and I found in golf a new common ground, something that sealed the bond in our friendship. The game was his greatest obsession, and I wanted to be able to share it with him. I am so thankful I made the effort.

But then, out of the blue, in 1993 a lucrative job offer came along in the form of a syndicated television series, to be filmed at Disneyworld in Orlando, Florida. Though my wife, Gina, and I had spoken about possibly wanting to raise our children in the country — for a number of different reasons, not the least of which was the whole "Hollywood-star's-kid" thing — we loved L.A. and we loved our lives there, our wonderful friends, and of course, being near Pop. It would be wretched to have to pack up and leave, but the Florida gig was such a sweet deal at such an appropriate time, it was almost impossible to say no.

So here I was at choice time again. I'd abandoned my dreams of being a classical pianist to pursue a career as an actor, which in my mind meant being a "serious" actor. And now here I was thinking of going to Disneyworld to shoot a TV series titled *Thunder in Paradise* with legendary wrestler Hulk Hogan. Clearly, we would not be doing *Hamlet.*

I knew the decision to leave Hollywood and take on a show like *Thunder* probably would put an end to the decent little career I'd created for myself, and that made the initial decision of whether or not to sign on a difficult one.

The upside was just too sweet, however. The show was projected to have a nice five- or six-year run, meaning the family and I could make a pretty penny while wintering at Disneyworld and summering in our New England country home. Not a bad life.

So finally, with only minor misgivings, we made the move to the East Coast, with Gina finding the house of our dreams in New England, located near some of the best schools in the country, while I traveled down to the Disney-MGM Studios in Florida, where I'd stay from January to June.

It turned out that the show had good production values and was an instant hit. Great news! Right choice! I'm a success!

Not so fast. After all, this is show business. One day that summer, Gina summoned me in from my beloved New England garden. It was a phone call from someone on the production staff, calling to tell me the gig was up. I heard something about money not flowing properly, and the network not caring about ratings; I heard that they'd already warned the producers, and blah, blah, blah . . .

My head dropped into my hands. I'd failed as a concert pianist. My so-called acting career had been a bust. What next? I wondered. Golf pro? Fore!

One thing I've learned about the biz part of show biz is that you better be out there rooting for yourself, because no one else is gonna do it for you. I've always suffered from a little lack of self-esteem, one result of the whole object-not-person thing, but I still have a good support system going, I like to work hard, and, most important, I thank God every day that I've been blessed with a wife and family that truly give my life meaning. So now it was time to put all that positive stuff to the test. We were staying in New England, a place that seemed a dream come true, and for me it was time once more to spin the big wheel of choices.

Acting had been great to me. Pop had been supportive of my career choice, but I'd never even considered asking him to do any favors for me professionally, and he'd never offered. Over time I'd had some nice bits in movies, and big roles in a few TV series, but I'd never found that big break I was looking for, and I was beginning to think the only way I was going to find it was to create it myself. So though I knew the odds were stacked heavily against me, I decided to try my hand at the "most likely not to succeed" business in the world, worse even than acting: being a writer.

And just as I'd done every time before when I started out in something new, I worked and studied and scratched. I wrote and wrote and rewrote. And I know now that writing is an art that I will never completely master, that there are new things to learn each day — and that actually is one of the things that makes it so much fun. But I also know that role, the big one I always looked for, is just around the corner.

A happy night at the Kennedy
Center Honors.

With Gina at the AFI tribute to Pop,
the night Shirley MacLaine and I
performed a Gershwin tune for him.

Chapter Eighteen

It was too late. I was too late.

While I was flying the red-eye cross-country that night, the demon pneumonia returned. Again Pop lay unconscious in bed. Again I sat, held his hand, and looked down at his face.

In just the short time I'd been gone, the cancer had accelerated, leaving his cheeks hollowed and his skin color jaundiced. Death was inevitable now, just a matter of waiting.

But there was so much I still wanted to say to him. I wanted to reminisce with him, laugh with him again, thank him from the bottom of my heart for all the things he'd given me, all the things we'd shared. I wanted to thank him for the magic. If only he could be here with me, just one more time. But I knew now that would never happen.

RITUALS

I'd spent hours talking to Gina, huddled in a corner at the far side of the courtyard that led to the cancer center, my cell phone pressed to my ear, a wad of tissues clenched in my fist.

Mom had been right about Gina — she'd been the perfect medicine to break the dark side of the Lemmon Legacy. The decade-plus we'd spent together had strengthened our bond, and in that time we'd produced three beautiful children, whom we adored beyond all comprehension. We'd created a home and a family together, and because of her instinctive wisdom, we'd been able to give our children what I never had: a mother and father at the dinner table, every night; a mother and father together, bonded, in a functioning union. And I'd been able to give my kids the one thing I'd missed the most — a father who was actively a part of their lives, an alpha male to depend on, to learn from, to trust.

Not that I didn't trust Pop, of course, and not that I didn't learn a hell of lot from him, didn't depend on him from time to time. Despite the divorce, despite the problems that cropped up between me and his second wife, despite having to share him with the rest of the world, he had loomed incredibly large in my life. And now he was going away. I was losing the guy I'd pulled out of Jimmy Coburn's koi pond, walked with down the hallowed fairways of Pebble Beach, looked up to as we cruised the finger lakes of southern Alaska. There wouldn't be any more wild rides in precious Porsches, or cheery, irreverent but ever-optimistic greetings on my phone machine ("Hey, Ramhead, go fuck yourself!"). He was going, and that was that.

In this age of miracles, fathers aren't supposed to die at seventy-six, that's too young. I'd lost Mom at sixty-two, and that was criminal, but seventy-six was still too young.

None of us had seen the end coming so quickly, least of all me; we'd all remained in a state of utter denial. And now it was too late to tell him those things I needed so badly to say.

So I found myself letting it all hang out for my beautiful wife, who listened patiently to every word as she held our world together a continent away. We talked into the night.

In addition to seeking approval from their fathers for actions well done, sons seek their approval as well when they become a man. This rite of passage has been ritualized in countless cultures across the world for thousands of years, but generally has faded from the picture in modern American society, especially when divorce is involved.

In earlier times, generations of families would live together in one unit, and young men were given a chance to see how their fathers and father's fathers would interact, which led to a clear transition to manhood. With the loss of that unity, there is no basic example for that passage, no road signs to help the young man along the way to achieving adulthood and to assuming all its responsibilities.

I think that on an instinctive level Pop understood that need, and I think that was the driving force behind our adventures together, those magical times when we would explore new realms. But when you're young, those times together go so quickly, and much of what makes up the fabric of that young boy's life is the memory of the long months between.

I know Pop tried, and I tried too, but

gone is gone, and no matter how much love there was when we were together, and no matter how many good times there were, they were never enough. The memory of that empty chair at the dinner table will be with me until my final days.

I had to end the phone call. It was getting late, and I wanted to go up and see Pop again before heading to the hotel. I told Gina I loved her and missed her, and that we weren't really sure, but the end probably was going to come soon.

Both of us paused for a minute and quietly cried. Then I whispered, "I love you," and moved to flip my cell phone closed, but stopped when I heard her voice calling out.

"Wait!"

"What?" I said.

"I love you too," she said back. "And happy birthday."

Chapter Nineteen

A CHANGE OF LIFE

Making the break from the life I'd known in Hollywood and moving East was not as difficult as I had feared. In truth, taking the job on *Thunder* was just part of the reason for my move. Yes, the money was good, but I was also tired of the rut I'd gotten in, both career-wise and personally. I had my own life now, my own family, and my own dreams. I'd had success, maybe not at Pop's level, but twenty years of straight work is a blessing for anyone in this business. The limelight had been good to me, but now I had something more, something bigger. I had a wonderful wife and family, and they were more impor-tant to me than anything Hollywood and show business had to offer. I would not make the same decisions and, to my mind anyway, the same mistakes as my father.

But then, of course, I was not my father. I would never be the "everyman" to a world of moviegoers. Jack Lemmon was owned by the world. I was too protective of the little world I had created for myself to ever let that happen to me.

The decision, then, to move away from Hollywood, followed by the decision to abandon what career I had as an actor and instead to try my hand as a writer, all seemed part of a greater plan, of one step leading logically to another. I loved to write — loved the whole process of creating something from nothing, of creating whole new worlds from a blank piece of paper. And I loved my family more than life itself. I was convinced that what I was doing was right. My resolve, however, didn't keep the shift from being difficult, even at times traumatic. Again, it was the memories.

Like when I stood in the living room of our Hollywood Hills house, looking from my balcony out over the sprawling city as the movers lowered my dear old Yamaha grand piano to the street below. The thin metal cable that they used hardly looked strong enough to hold the piano, much less the weight of all the memories attached to it. Memories of all the great nights when Pop and I played together, many of them special, like the party we had after our first Pebble Beach Tournament, when we jammed with Peter Jacobsen, Mark O'Meara, and a very patient Bruce Hornsby on the keys.

One thing Gina and I had learned from my dear mother was how to fill a house with joy and parties, and our soulful old house just screamed for them. Built in 1921 as a club for men who sought the horizontal company of women — i.e., a whorehouse — our home was situated at the base of the Santa Monica Mountains, and climbed four stories up the hill on which it was built. Whether it was the ghosts of those notorious ladies and their clients, or the energy of another of the house's former owners, Gary Cooper, Gina and I both felt that it was our duty to keep the place filled with as much fun as possible.

Pop loved the house too, frequently dropping by for spur-of-the-moment visits. As he had in the ocean room at Mom's beach house, he'd go up to the third-floor living room that looked out over the city and sit at the piano, playing Gershwin and chilling for hours on end. He also loved the terraced sandstone garden I'd built up behind the fourth floor, the one that was so reminiscent of the Beverly Glen house.

One thing he didn't love, though — and he wasn't shy letting me know about it — was a huge elephant plant I'd placed on the front porch. Truth is, it really was hideous, something I'd bought at a market downtown during a moment of delirium. It bugged Pop so much, though, I just had to keep it around. Virtually every time he left our house, he would drive out of his way, just so he could pass the porch again and scream, "Hate that plant!"

There was a lot I left behind when I moved away from Hollywood. The memories went with me, of course, but most of the people and just about all of the lifestyle that had fostered those memories would no longer be a part of my life, just as I would no longer be a part of that world.

Intrinsic as it was, though, my desire to become a writer wasn't at the heart of my decision to make such a drastic change. There was the dawning realization that, in my life, something was missing. Something was broken, deep down inside. And I needed to fix it.

Becoming a father had been a revelation for me, a sobering, eye-opening wake-up call to grow up and take responsibility for helping to bring to life these amazing creatures Gina and I had been blessed with. I'd had a Hollywood childhood, and as great as it was at times, and as wonderful as it is to be able to tell these stories about it now, it wasn't something I wanted my kids to go through. Being elbowed aside by well-meaning but overly excited autograph seekers — being identified as an object, not a person — or seeing that empty chair at the dinner table: these would not be for my children.

Of course, my family had broken apart when I was very young, and I was certain that would never happen to Gina and me. But "Hollywood divorce" aside, a Hollywood childhood was not necessarily the best preparation for dealing with the real world. I wanted my kids to have it all — to know and to love and to respect everything their grandfather, and their father, had accomplished, but I wanted them to have their own lives as well — independent of him, independent of me. With this realization, leaving for New England seemed the best action I could take.

Our first child, Sydney Noel, was actually a Hollywood baby; her brothers, Christopher Jr. and Jonathan, were Connecticut born. And, appropriately, Sydney's arrival gave rise to one of the classic Lemmon Legacy stories: Just as Gina was going through the actual final moments of delivery, Pop, with perfect timing, had strutted into the hospital room, where he found Gina yelping, our OB-GYN, Ed Liu, yelling "PUSH!" and me Lamaze-ing like mad. I shouted a distracted, "Hey, Lem," over the curtain and noted a look of horror on Pop's face. Ten minutes later found Gina and me glowing as we looked down at our beautiful Syd, and then there was a realization — where's Pop?

Gina looked around, called out, "Pop?"

A moan came from around the corner. I went over to investigate and found Pop hooked up to oxygen and a blood-pressure monitor, Ed Liu waving smelling salts under his nose. Ed looked up at me and said, "You guys did great, wish I could say the same for Jack."

Waking up the next day, I was filled with a mixture of emotions. Elation was paramount among them, but anxiety had claimed a spot as well. I was determined to be a good father, to give my daughter all the time and attention she could want or need. But the truth was, I didn't know how. Parenting skills, alas, were not a part of the Lemmon Legacy.

AN AMERICAN LEGACY IN PARIS

My father truly adhered to the New England ethic of "the son does it on his own." (Not to mention that other powers in his household would never allow it any other way.) But he had put me through college, and bought me an ancient Oldsmobile; and he'd loaned me a few bucks on the sly during my first lean years out of Cal Arts. Then, after I got my first real job, taking over for Ted Danson as "The Aramis Man," I'd written a check for five thousand dollars as repayment and handed it to him, fully expecting him to say, "Don't worry about it, kiddo, you hold on to it." Instead he grabbed the check and said, "Thanks, Ramhead, lunch on me!"

Despite his inclination to let me fend for myself, though, one thing Pop loved and always shared with me were his great trips. Okay, admittedly once I was grown I had to pay for them, but what the hell, they were still great.

Right before Papa Jack died, Pop had taken him on a tour of Europe. Pop later said that the trip turned out to be the single most enlightening time in their relationship, the first chance they'd had to be friends. After a lifetime of their guarded relationship, they'd finally cut loose and had a great time together. Pop had a lot of stories about that trip, but there was one that he relished in particular:

He and Papa Jack had finished a great day in Venice and had both supposedly gone up to their rooms for the night. But there must have been something in the air that evening, because Pop, restless, later found himself wandering the streets, eventually catching a gondola for a midnight ride. As he floated around a corner, another gondola across the way attracted his attention.

As Pop strained forward, he realized it wasn't the gondola itself that caught his eye, but its occupants, a man and a woman who seemed strangely familiar. In typical Legacy form, as he scrambled forward to get a closer look, he almost fell into the canal.

Gliding toward him from the opposite direction was a distinguished older gentleman with a knockout young honey nestled on his arm. And as the two boats passed in the night, the older gentleman turned, tipped his bowler, smiled, and winked at his gaping son. Yes indeed, it had been Papa Jack.

"What a pistol!" Pop used to say about his father after that evening. It was too bad he'd found it out so late in Papa Jack's life, because a short while later he would be gone. But it was great that he'd gotten the chance to break through the barriers that had been set up in their relationship and finally just be friends.

Pop and I had our trip to Europe as well, very much like the one he took with Papa Jack, but with one intrinsic difference — the Lemmon Legacy factor had grown even stronger . . .

My dear sister Courtney had courageously volunteered to come along on this particular journey, so it was the three of us in Paris for a week, hitting every museum, park, and boulangerie we could find. And the truly amazing thing was, during all our outings for that entire week, Pop and I somehow managed to keep the Legacy at bay. Neither of us had fallen in the River Seine, or gotten impaled on the spires of Notre Dame; we hadn't jettisoned an espresso at the musée du Louvre, or knocked over the ovens at Le Coq Hardi. On the contrary, it actually looked as though we were going to make it out of France without a single Legacy mishap. But now, as I look back on the way things played out, I realize it wasn't that we'd escaped the Legacy, it was just that the Legacy was saving everything up for one last big night.

On our final evening, Pop treated us to

dinner at one of the finest restaurants in Paris. We arrived at dusk and were seated at a terrific table overlooking the city.

Now there's one trait I have that hasn't been mentioned so far, and since it is salient to this story, there's no point in holding back any longer: I'll eat just about anything. It's something that Pop knew and delighted in, he himself being more than a little particular about what he would allow into his stomach.

Pop used to love to take me along to his favorite haunts, like Frascatti's or the Brown Derby, way back when, and get a bunch of his friends together to watch me eat clams on the half-shell, steak tartar, or escargot. I think it was kind of a 1950s version of *Fear Factor* for them.

Anyway, ever since arriving in Paris, I'd been dying to go to this particular restaurant I'd heard about, the one that served a famous dish the name of which translated from the French as something like "duck in its own sauce." To my way of thinking, anything in its own sauce had to be given a try, and this was one dish I was determined would not go untested. And somehow (perhaps having something to do with the perky little Bourgogne we'd sampled at cocktail hour), I'd talked Pop into giving the duck a try as well.

However, despite my efforts to dissuade her, Courtney ordered the lamb. I tried to convince her that just plain old lamb wasn't worthy of a restaurant of this caliber, and that you only get to eat in a place like this a few times in your life, so if there was ever a time she should go out on a limb and get some duck, this was it. She stood firm, however, while Pop and I went for the gold.

All through the appetizer (I'm not too good with French, but I think mine had something to do with cow's lips), I spoke of the duck. I'd done my research, reading about how they take the carcass of the duck and crush it in a press — an ancient press, one dating back centuries, centuries of duck-carcass pressing — and in a time-honored tradition had turned duck in its own sauce into a culinary work of art. And then the moment came — the trays were wheeled out and two giant burnished-copper serving ovens were revealed.

We sat in reverent silence as the ritual of the serving of the duck unfolded. First though, a small, unassuming waiter placed a plate of perfectly prepared lamb in front of Courtney. Then two extremely stern-looking waiters marched from behind thick velvet curtains and bowed to Pop and me. Pop stammered a perfectly Lemmon acknowledgment ("Uhh-bu-ehheps-uh-*merci!*"), and the reveal took place.

With a flourish, the burnished-copper ovens were opened, the sea of waiters and waiters' assistants parted, and the world-famous duck in its own sauce was set before us.

Pop and I looked down — and then there was a long pause.

In front of us sat two plain white bowls, filled with what looked like bacon covered in brown Jell-O.

There was another long pause; then Pop looked up and said, "That's it?"

I quickly turned to the horrified waiters, exclaiming, "That's it all right! And aren't we excited, my father and me! See? Look at him!"

The waiters looked over at Pop who still sat staring at the plate. Noting the growing look of bewilderment on his face, they bustled away, saying indecipherable things amongst themselves.

Pop immediately turned to me: "Whattaya, trying to kill me?"

"Pop, hold it down," I admonished. "They're watching us!" Truthfully, though, when I examined the meal before me, even

I had doubts — this was one scary-looking dish.

I glanced over at Pop, who was now stabbing at the duck with his knife, a queer expression of disgust and intrigue on his face. Then I checked out the waiters in the corner, all of them still watching us, contempt written all over their faces.

"Pop, seriously," I whispered, "you're gonna give these guys a heart attack. This stuff's holy to them!"

But now Pop's eyes had shifted to the plate that sat in front of his beloved daughter. He watched with longing as she gently carved through her beautifully prepared lamb, lying on its bed of wild rice and freshly picked forest mushrooms.

"How's the lamb, sweetie?" he asked, his smile a bit too stiff.

"Absolutely delicious," she responded, smiling back.

"Good, that's good," he said sweetly. Then he turned to me: "You're disowned."

One of the stern-looking waiters approached our table. Turning to Courtney, he asked, "Is everything prepared to your liking, Madam?"

"Perfectly," she responded, smiling up at him.

The waiter then turned slowly to Pop

and me. "Eh Messieurs?"

"Actually, now that you mention it . . ." Pop started.

". . . We're as pleased as punch," I finished. "How about another glass of wine? Make it two for Mr. Lemmon."

The waiter moved away and Pop turned to me. "You're a ghost — out of the estate entirely."

"Oh for God's sake, Pop, they've been making this crap for thousands of years, so there's got to be something to it. I'm going to give it a try."

Pop grinned a particularly evil grin. "That's m'boy."

And then I looked down at the duck in its own sauce, and for the first time in my life questioned my own resolve. With determination, however, I set myself to the task, slowly raising a forkful of the mysterious-looking dish to my lips.

I realized suddenly that I now had the attention not only of Pop and Courtney and the assembled waiters; the entire restaurant was focused on me and the bit of food on my now-trembling fork. Silence reigned.

As I carefully lifted the duck to my mouth, I noticed there was no scent at all — no hint of coriander, no dash of thyme.

No, this duck was of a whole different universe de cuisine. In retrospect, I believe that chewing that bite of duck in its own sauce may have been the bravest thing I've ever done.

I looked up from the duck, then over at Pop, who stared back and then tilted his head, appearing not unlike a curious cocker spaniel. Then I turned to the stern-looking waiters, called on my deepest acting chops, swallowed, and gave them the thumbs-up.

Instantly the waiters were all over Pop and me, fawning, and speaking hymns of the duck. And, like a cleansing wind, the tension in the room, so palpable just moments before, seemed to vanish, the mood becoming instantly jubilant.

Pop beamed, put his arm around my shoulder, and announced, "What a champ!" Then he pushed his bowl of duck in its own sauce in front of me. "Here, have another."

After experiencing duck in its own sauce, we couldn't just go back to the hotel, or at least Pop and I couldn't. No, the fires of the duck would need to be quenched, so, after saying good night to Courtney, we headed to the world-famous Folies

Bergere. Now that it was behind us, I was sure that the duck experience would be our only brush with the Lemmon Legacy for this trip, but, of course, I was wrong. I should have known that with Pop and me together for a week, the one episode would not be enough to satisfy our curse. And, sure enough, after the show at the Folies Bergere, and after several helpings of the most delicious champagne I've ever tasted, the Legacy struck again.

Post showtime, fully in the spirit, Pop and I went backstage to congratulate the performers, at which point a rehearsing can-can dancer kicked one of us in the head. I don't remember which one of us suffered the blow, but suffice it to say that the rest of that evening's activities seemed to take on an ethereal, otherworldly aspect.

Bruised, battered, and bordering on nauseated, we managed to catch a cab whose driver didn't speak English, and since neither Pop nor I could figure out the French term for "nightclub," he finally ended up driving us to a whorehouse, something we did not realize, of course, until we were inside.

The next thing we knew we were all alone in a very scary place, sitting at a sleazy bar with two birdlike, very thin, scantily-clad women and a huge, petulant bodyguard. And now, probably due in part to the trauma from my head injury, the tables had turned and *I* was the one doing the complaining while Pop struggled to cover our tracks.

"Five hundred bucks for this bottle of dishwater! Are these guys nuts?!" I barked, staring down at the cheap American champagne in front of us.

Pop shushed me. "Relax, hotshot, the Crane Sisters are coming back!"

Sure enough the two ladies of the evening were being ushered back toward us by the surly bodyguard, who didn't look at all happy.

Pop whipped around, whispered emphatically, "Look, give the guy the $500 and let's get the hell outta here, before we get our kneecaps busted!"

"Why am I always the one who has to pay?" I asked petulantly.

But my supplications were to no avail. After emptying both our wallets, we politely declined offered favors, and the predawn skies found Pop and me, too broke to get a cab, hoofing it out of the red-light district and finally arriving at the River Seine.

Halfway across the bridge and with our hotel in sight, Pop stopped, sat down, and rubbed his feet. I sat next to him and looked about.

"Beautiful, isn't it?"

"Shut up," he growled. "Rotten kid. What a mess you got me into."

I smiled. "I gotta tell you, Pop, I have more fun with you than anybody else in the world."

"If you call what we've been through tonight 'fun,' then you're sicker than I thought," he said, giving me an elbow.

But I had meant it. Despite the Lemmon Legacy — or maybe because of it — when we were together, Pop and I always had the time of our lives.

We continued to have those wonderful and manic adventures together, at least until his later years, when we seemed to drift apart again. I wondered if the emotional distance was caused by my move to New England, or if this was a natural progression in the parent-child relationship, something that happened as both parties grew older. I wondered also if this was a product of the whole Hollywood divorce son-of-the-first-marriage syndrome, or if it was, quite simply, another part of the Legacy.

It wasn't until after Pop was gone, however, that I began to get a grasp on the answers to those questions, raising yet more that I found myself wanting to ask him, wanting to have the chance to better understand this man I loved so much, questions I held onto until it was too late. Questions that I realize now will never be answered.

I began my life going down the same path as my father. Circumstances and time changed all that, as I wandered off in another direction — finding love and lasting companionship, starting a family, becoming a writer, moving to Connecticut. Yet my father was always there, and his path was always open to me. But now that option was gone, and there would be no going back. I was losing my best friend. I was losing my father.

Chapter Twenty

THE BIG PICTURE ENDS

The sun sat thick and burning red on the smoggy horizon, giving everything a somber, almost unearthly glow. The rush-hour traffic had turned downtown L.A. into a parking lot, and as I sat high atop an overpass in my rental car, making my way east toward the cancer center, I remember looking out at my beloved city — my birth-place, my home for almost a half century — and not recognizing it at all.

As with most kids, the eyes of my youth were veiled in innocence, but unlike now, the times had been more innocent as well. I'd grown up on the beaches of Santa Monica when there were still bat caves in the hills and not just wall-to-wall houses, when the intersection of Laurel and Ventura was orange groves instead of a twenty-four-hour traffic jam, when I could ride my Sting-Ray bike up the Pacific Coast Highway to grade school. All that

One of my last pictures with Pop.

was gone now, all those times and places, gone — but not the memories.

As I sat, high over the 101 Freeway, the roads around me packed with thousands of cars as far as the eye could see, I thought back over what I'd had, and what I'd lost. In a lifetime we're confronted with so many choices, so many possible paths. There were some wrong turns in mine, of course, but overall I'd had a fairly smooth journey. And there were some regrets, naturally, but not too many, and none of them ran too deep.

However, now, as my time with Pop drew to a close, I'd finally realized one very big regret: despite all our times spent together, all our adventures, travels, and travails, I'd never sat down, looked him in the eye, and told him just how very much he meant to

me. Perhaps he knew it; perhaps he understood. But still, it was something I now
wished I'd said.

I reached the hospital room and found
Pop alone, which was unusual; these days
he was attended to pretty much around the
clock. He was asleep, and I pulled up a
chair, moving next to the bed, grateful for
this opportunity to have him all to myself,
to have it be just us boys, if only for a moment, if only in silence.

Scenes from our lives together played
out in my mind, and I swallowed back a
half-laugh, half-sob. I'd been doing a lot of
reminiscing these last few days, almost as if
the big screen in my head was running the
end credits reel; all those outtakes, buried
so deeply, were leaping forward as I
unspooled the memories. I confess it had
been difficult showing up these last few
weeks, knowing that the end was so close
at hand. Of course I wanted to see Dad,
but I wanted to see the vital, vibrant man
who'd taken me fishing, played piano with
me till dawn; I wanted the man who'd been
my golfing buddy, my drinking partner —
my best friend. I wanted the chance to say
those words I'd somehow never managed
to say. Now it was too late.

The setting sun filled the room with an orange glow, as the day slipped steadily away. The only sound in the room was the slow, steady beeps of the battery of instruments monitoring Pop's vital functions as they gradually weakened. It wouldn't be long now.

I wanted to rail against the whole thing, wanted to scream to the heavens that this man who'd brought joy, laughter, heartbreak, and decades of memories to millions, couldn't leave like this, so quietly, hidden away in a tiny hospital room. No, this event demanded grandeur — an Arthurian funeral, high atop a brilliantly lit mountain. A touching death scene, as the king slides slowly to his final rest.

I leaned forward and took Pop's hand, so thin now, the skin almost transparent. As I had countless times before, I took a wet towel and gently wiped his forehead, soothing myself more than him, speaking softly to the man I adored, my father.

"It's me, Pop," I whispered. "Just got back from sushi. I ordered the giant clam balls, just for you. Got a bunch of other disgusting stuff too, you would've loved it. While I was eating I remembered that time on one of our first trips to Alaska, when we'd gone out to dinner at that new Japanese place in Anchorage. After we were seated you'd gone to the can, and while you were in there they brought us a huge bowlful of raw herring eggs on seaweed for an appetizer. You came out and saw Kay and me knocking 'em back and thought we were eating pickles, so you grabbed a huge piece and downed it, and I swear to God Pop . . . Your face . . ."

I looked down at him, still there but so far away.

"Maybe we'll do it again one of these days, huh, Pop? Some other place, some other time, maybe we'll get a chance to nail a tee shot, or catch a monster trout together again. I hope so, Pop, I truly do."

More memories raced through my mind, moments trapped in time, recalled now as though they happened yesterday.

"Remember that summer when I decided to play baseball with the little league? You came to every one of my games, even though I stunk out loud, you came, and sat, and grimaced. All season long I never got one hit, but you still came. You even took me to the batting cages each weekend and practiced with me, still no hit.

"Finally, last inning of the last game, two down, last man up, the coach is forced to put me at bat. I beg him not to, so do the rest of the team, but fair play and all . . . So I get up to the plate, the team's last hope, and I look over at you with your huge Cuban cigar hanging out of your mouth, and you motion, 'relax,' just like you'd done a dozen times before at the cages.

"The first pitch is inside and almost takes my head off — of course, I mug to the bleachers for a laugh. Us Lemmon Boys could always get one of those when we were playing sports, couldn't we? I take an impossible swing at the next pitch, and then the one after. Now it's truth time — one more swing to end the season. And right before the pitch, I look over at you, and you flash me the old Lemmon smile, the one that says, 'Maybe next year, kiddo.' And I smile back, turn, and hit a ripper, just like that. Everyone is so stupefied, they all just stand there and watch the ball bounce off the left-field wall — me included. Then everybody realizes what I've done, and they start screaming, 'Run . . . Run!!' so I do. It was the first time you'd ever seen me run the bases, and you later said I looked like a drunk spider. I was so slow they actually threw me out at second, but you didn't care: you were so proud of me for hitting that damn ball, you wouldn't stop talking about it all day — and that meant so much to me, Pop . . . It meant so much.

"I see the same thing in my boys. I can't tell you what it's been like to be there, every day, watching them grow, going to their soccer matches, their baseball games, watching them turn into little men, turn into my best friends.

"I know you never really understood, Pop, but that's why I had to get out when I did. I wanted them to have what I couldn't, and I needed to be the one there giving it to them. I know business had to come first for you. After a while you had no choice, you didn't belong to me or to any one person anymore — the world had laid claim to Jack Lemmon, and I want you to know, I understood that. But that wasn't me. I did have a choice, and I chose to be with my family. I had to put them first.

"What we did together, Pop — those unbelievable adventures, those other worlds — I'll never forget them. They were some of the greatest times of my life, and I'll carry them with me forever.

"I'll carry you with me, forever.

"I love you, Pop.

"Good-bye."

I was grateful for the private time I'd had with Pop, which ended just as the glow of the L.A. sunset faded from the room. Pop's three nurses, who over the last year had become like family to all of us, came back from dinner and stopped by to see him. Gradually we were joined by other family members, and then by the usual contingency of doctors and staff.

The mood in the room soon lightened, as people formed small groups and engaged in animated conversation. The starkness of the space was replaced with a warmth that transformed the room in a spiritual way, brightening everything.

Then Louise, one of the three nurses who had ministered to Pop so lovingly in these final months, came up to me and put a hand on my shoulder. Looking up at me with her kind blue eyes, she quietly whispered, "He's taking his leave now."

The moments that followed seemed to be held in suspension, a world devoid of time and motion. The memories came flooding back as I crossed to say one more farewell to this man who had hung the moon in my world.

"Okay, Slick, give it your best shot. Oh, and watch out for that trap on the left . . ."

I knelt next to the bed and embraced my father for the last time, pulling him close to me.

"Man! This thing's fast," he shouts as he drives my Porsche a hundred miles an hour down Sunset Boulevard, gears grinding, his face one big, wild-eyed smile.

"I love you, Pop . . ."

"Two Irish guys walk out of a pub . . . Hey it could happen!" Kay, Rick, and I all roar with laughter, happy to bask in the glow of this amazing man, happy to be together on a riverbank in Alaska. And then our laughter becomes uncontrollable as a huge tug on Pop's fly line yanks him headfirst into the stream . . .

"I'll never forget."

"A second dram of the elixir of pine-tar and nicotine, barkeep. And while you're at it bring another round of snails for Ramhead here . . ."

"I love you."

"Here we go, kiddo . . ."

"I'll never forget."

"Magic time!"

Pop stands in the trap near the eighteenth hole, a look of determination combined with abject prayer on his face, as his sand-shot arcs upward. Then, as it dives, bites, and slowly spins down the tabletop green toward the hole, his face transforms into a display of absolute elation. He

229

pumps his fist and screams over the bellowing gallery, "Now that's a touch of terrific!" And then the strut, that Jack Lemmon strut, as he marches into another year at Pebble, another hopeful stab at the elusive Dragon . . .

"I love you."

"Quiet," he whispers. "Don't make a sound." I look where he's pointing, and sure enough, there in the murky wee-hours light of James Coburn's backyard stand Walter and Virgil, the French poodles from hell. Pop slowly turns to me, a full-blown Professor Fate expression on his amazing face, and says, "Let's kick their fuzzy asses!" And we're off . . .

"I'll never forget."

I'm eleven years old, cruising the finger lakes of southern Alaska at the end of the most magical week of my life. I've seen and done things that before I'd only dreamed of, and they have changed me forever. I've also learned a life-altering lesson by coming to a realization that I don't have to constantly seek approval, that thing I always felt I needed from Pop. In fact, it's been there all along, unconditionally and unequivocally, a truth unspoken, a part of the bond between father and son — the love.

I look up at my father and he says, "I want you to know, I'll always be there for you. Don't ever forget that."

"I'll never forget."

"I love you, kiddo."

"I love you, Pop . . ."

"I'll never forget."

On the evening of June 27, 2001, my father, Jack Lemmon, the world's everyman, passed away in my arms.

The world will always have him, seen in his glory, a man of many faces and souls, his talent on record for generations to come.

But I'll carry a much different part of him with me, a side of the man that only I saw, this man who gave me some of the greatest memories of my life, a father's gift to his son.

I love you, Pop. Always.

I'll never forget.

Chapter Twenty-One

HOLLYWOOD PIXELS

Though writing this book was a cathartic experience for me, it didn't make it any easier to handle those feelings of loss that come from time to time; the time I spent with Pop in reminiscence, however, did in some small way help to heal the deep loss I felt. I adored my father, and it seems I'm not alone in that. Aside from his enormous talent, Pop seemed to touch every heart he came near. This was a loved man, a man who made the world a little brighter for all those around him, and a man who is sorely missed but remembered with great joy, not only by me, but by his dear friends as well.

I am deeply touched to have had the opportunity to invite these friends and colleagues to share in this special chapter that ends my tribute to Pop and to fill it with their bright light, with their fine tales, with their shared love for this special man. He gave us all many gifts, but as I read these heartfelt remembrances from these very special people, I am reassured that he gave us all one gift in common: magic. And when you were with Jack Lemmon, it was always "Magic time."

NEIL SIMON

I don't remember how many films I wrote for Jack Lemmon, but I know it wasn't enough. I gladly would have done it forever.

Jack astounded me, always. For example, there was a scene in *The Prisoner of Second Avenue* in which Mel — that was the character Jack played — went out on his Manhattan apartment balcony and brayed at the world, giving vent to his anger at losing his longtime job due to a failing economy, and to his frustration at the level of noise coming from the neighboring apartment (stewardesses entertaining pilots — this was the 1970s, remember). Of course, this was not the first time Mel had gone out on his balcony overlooking Second Avenue and screamed at the world, and as far as his upstairs neighbor was concerned, this was one time too many. All Mel really wanted was peace and a little sympathy; what he got was a bucketful of cold water right in his face, a kind of ultimate humiliation. Finally defeated, Mel walked slowly back into the room, where his wife dried his hair with a towel, and tried to console him with tea and sympathy.

In the film, Jack played this scene simply but so very effectively. The world had just crashed in on him, but instead of another great display of emotion, he allowed the thought of what had just happened to flow through his mind, and instead of tears, a sad, wry smiled flickered across his face as the lunacy of it sank in. He tried to say something, but no sound came out as his wife lovingly tried to dry his wet face and head. On screen, it was a thirty-second moment, but it played out like *Death in Venice* — brilliant and moving and defining. In thirty seconds, Jack made us know and understand that man, and love and respect him too. Watching it, I thought that he must have drawn on some deep well of sadness from his own youth — it was that real. But I wasn't surprised, because Jack had it all.

I also loved his dedication to his craft. During scene breaks, while the lights were rearranged for the next shot, most of the other actors would get a Coke or call their agent, but not Jack. Jack always — and I do mean *always* — sat and prepared for the next scene, going over his lines, mentally making the character come alive. It was as though Picasso was painting in his head, and you knew instinctively to leave him alone. A DO NOT DISTURB sign couldn't have been more effective.

When I first went to Hollywood from New York, the legendary agent Swifty Lazar threw a party in my honor. In attendance were people like Fred Astaire, Gregory Peck, Billy Wilder, Rosalind Russell, Natalie Wood — virtually every major film star, director, and writer who *could* be there *was* there. But unless Lazar tapped them on the shoulder to introduce me, I was ignored. None of them approached me, tried to make me feel welcome. None except Jack Lemmon. If I remember correctly, he was on the way to the loo, drink in hand, when he stopped and smiled at me and said, "How you doin', kid?" and put his hand on my shoulder. That was it, but for me it was everything, and he was the only one that night who actually spoke to me. Right there, I promised myself, "I will dedicate my life to him."

Of the films Jack and I worked on together, *The Out-of-Towners* was one of my favorites. I remember that when I first wrote it, it was just a draft of a new play, and in no shape to show anyone, especially a star of Jack Lemmon's standing. So on the day that I had lunch with him to discuss the possibility of involving him in the project, I had no script; I just wanted to tell Jack about it for future reference. As I sat there talking, it suddenly occurred to me that there I was pitching an unwritten idea to Jack Lemmon, and that he was far too big a star for me to be offering so little. Yet I plowed ahead, knowing I had to say more than "How's your shrimp salad?"

When I finished talking, I said to Jack, "Well, that's all I have, but I just wanted you to hear it." What I expected in response was, "Fine, Neil. When you write it, send it to me." But that's not what I heard at all. What Jack said instead was, "I like it. In fact, I love it. Let's do it!"

"Really?" I said, my mouth open in amazement. "You really like it?"

"Tell me when we start shooting and I'll be there." He got up, smiled, took a cookie, and left.

He was there on the first day of shooting, totally marvelous that day and every day. I remember watching him and thinking back to that first night I met him at Swifty Lazar's party, and his hand on my shoulder as he said, "How you doin', kid?"

I miss him desperately.

BLAKE EDWARDS

Some time ago a reporter from a national magazine asked me whom of all the actors that I had worked with did I admire most.

Without hesitation I replied, "If I were restricted to only one actor that I could work with for the rest of my career, without a doubt it would be Jack Lemmon."

ANDY GARCIA

I first met Jack Lemmon through his son Chris, who was and is one of my golfing partners and a dear friend. One day Chris called and invited me to play at Hillcrest Country Club in Los Angeles. He said, "We are going to play with my dad."

Play golf with his dad! With *THE* JACK LEMMON! I thought to myself.

"Let me check my schedule," I replied.

Chris laughed and said, "Don't worry, Pop is great."

Jack was not only an acting god, but to all of us amateur golfers, he was an institution as well. He exemplified total devotion to and love for the game. I had grown up watching him play at the AT&T, or the Crosby, if you go way back, so as you can see, this was a very special day for me.

When I arrived at Hillcrest, he was already on the driving range, trying to groove what many might describe lovingly as an ungroovable swing. But his concentration and love of the process was inspiring. Chris introduced us, and Jack gave me a warm welcome and immediately complimented me on my work. I was deeply touched, and immediately replied, "It is an honor to meet you, Mr. Lemmon. I am a great admirer."

"Thank you," he replied. "Now go ahead and hit a few and let's play." I guess he wanted to focus on what was most important — golf!

On the first tee he gave me the honors, and we hit away. My drive barely found the fairway, as my nerves got the best of me. The thought, *I'm playing golf with Jack Lemmon,* kept rattling in my brain.

Throughout the round, Jack was constantly funny, and I was cordial and well behaved. But then came the par five along Motor Avenue. I guess Jack had enough of my cordial behavior, and maybe had gotten a little tired of hearing, "Good shot, Mr. Lemmon," "Nice putt, Mr. Lemmon," and wanted to loosen things up a bit, because as I proceeded to slice my three wood second shot over the tall fence and into the afternoon traffic along Motor Avenue, I heard from behind me this loud cry: "Piece of shit!"

I turned around in the direction of the cry expecting to see Chris, but instead I saw Jack cupping his hands over his mouth and again screaming at the ball and proclaiming, "Piece of shit!" I laughed uncontrollably.

Many laughs followed throughout the rest of the day, as did, unfortunately, many more pieces of shit.

Some months later I was fortunate enough to be invited to play in the AT&T Pro-Am Tournament at Pebble Beach. It was my friend Mr. Lemmon who got me the invitation, through Clint Eastwood, another soon-to-be friend and a blessing in my life.

The first year I played in the pro-am, the last two rounds were rained out. The second year, the golf god touched my partner, Paul Stankowski, and me, and we won the tournament. When I got back to Los Angeles, I went again to Hillcrest to play, and there was Jack, hitting balls at the driving range. When I approached him, he gave me a big hug and said, "My hero!"

"That's my line," I replied.

He smiled, and in that moment I felt that he would have traded one of his Oscars for that AT&T trophy — a great deal for both of us.

I had the great honor of playing with Jack, in his foursome, in his last AT&T tournament. I know in my heart that he had made that happen. Our foursome consisted of Jack, his partner in time, Peter Jacobsen, my partner, Paul Stankowski, and me. Jack had in his bag as many woods as he had irons, and his caddie, Dave Pelz, was having him hit a wood from 150 yards out, and with that ungroovable swing, Jack was golfing the shit out of the ball.

"Good shot, Jack!" we shouted. "Great putt, Jack!" I, along with Peter and Paul and Dave, was totally engrossed in Jack's game. His determination and desire was inspirational. We were Jack's army that week, and if the last round hadn't been rained out, Jack Lemmon, one the greatest actors in history and someone I was proud to call my friend, after so many years of trying would have been playing on Sunday, in the final round of the AT&T Pro-Am. Jack Lemmon finally had made the cut! I was there.

Yes, I was there. But so was God. And God also wanted to play with Jack. After that year, Jack was taken from us. And to this day, whenever a friend hits a bad shot, I get this sudden urge to cup my hands over my mouth and proclaim at the top of my lungs, "Piece of shit!"

Jack Lemmon was an American original and a real class act, traits he passed on to his son, Chris. I loved Jack Lemmon, and I always felt he loved me back.

JULIE ANDREWS

My husband, Blake Edwards, phoned Jack one day to ask if he'd be interested in starring in a small, low-budget, experimental film that was to go before the cameras almost immediately. Jack's reply was, "Sure. When do we start?"

Within weeks we were filming in our own home, no less. Friends and family were working as a team, and we were all enjoying a new creative freedom.

The film was called *That's Life!* and Jack and I played Harvey and Gillian Fairchild — he an architect in full midlife crisis, about to celebrate his birthday, and I, a singer, secretly awaiting the results of a biopsy on tissue taken from her throat. Our real-life children played our family: Jack's son Chris played our son; my girls, Jennifer and Emma, played our daughters.

I'd known Jack as a friend for several years, and Blake often relayed to me the pleasure he had had working with him on previous films. Now I discovered that pleasure for myself, for Jack was a sublime actor — and utterly adorable.

I remember filming one evening in our

bedroom — a sweet scene filled with the intimacy that married couples share. Looking into Jack's eyes, I received the gift of his genuine, completely focused self. He made it so easy for me to respond; it was pure pleasure to share the moment with him.

The film became one of Blake's and my happiest working experiences, and Jack is simply front and center in all our memories of it.

Off camera, he was a member of our extended film family — without ego and self-effacing, playing our grand piano at every opportunity (quite wonderfully!) and regaling us with stories and chatting up the cast and crew, all of whom adored him.

After filming was over, he wrote me the loveliest letter, which I cherish.

I miss him very much.

TONY CURTIS

Jack and Me

As far back as I can remember,
    Jack and me were friends forever
He played the piano like a master
And the girls I played with, I was faster
The moments in our lives seemed
    to resemble each other
Between us all, the parts that came,
    only he and me could claim to play
The times we had, we had our joys
    and pain
Between us, parts were ours with fame
I would paint; he would draw
And tell each other tales before
We were always boys, don't you see
Stickball, marbles, cards,
    then climb a tree
Yes, Jack and me

My darling buddy and costar was one of the finest people in Hollywood, particularly because he was "normal." Yes, Jack was the "normal" star — no temperament, no ego, no tardiness, no outrageous ego-driven arguments, no vanity, and no self-centeredness.

Instead, his "normalcy" included punctuality, preparedness, cooperation, kindness, sensitivity, comic genius, and so much unparalleled talent that even Billy Wilder would ask for twenty more takes, just to watch and revel in Jack's ability to do it a different way each time. I would come in on my days off to witness this mutual admiration of masters.

In addition, his musical talent at the piano enriched his life and the lives of those of us around him.

Yes, Jack was extraordinary, yet "normal," a credit to the human species who strive to be "normal" like him. It was magic to be in his time and in his presence.

And when he went to bed at night, I'm sure the "purple throbber" was happy. At least Felicia said it was.

Jack Lemmon was to some a mystery — not in the usual sense, but a mystery as a survivor. Some how, some way, and with some remarkable survivability, Jack managed to trod the minefields of Hollywood with a nimble instinct. All the while, he was the quintessential "nice guy." The mystery, of course, is how do you remain a nice guy in a less-than-nice environment?

Decency comes to mind — inherent decency. But there was more. Some kind of Teflon allowed Jack to slide, slip, dodge, and flip. He was an "open field runner" in a less-than-open field. I think what he possessed went beyond survivability, though Jack was certainly aware of the tar pits and pitfalls in the "Land of La-La." Jack could dodge and swerve, all the while maintaining an integrity — his own brand.

I think Jack, like the Energizer Bunny, just kept on "going," never missing his step, never off in his timing. Focused, always focused on the finish line, Jack won his race — his own race, his personal race — and he did it his way, the only way he knew how. The decent way.

PETER JACOBSEN

I had the distinction and great pleasure of partnering with Jack Lemmon at the Pebble Beach Pro-Am Tournament from, I think, 1981 through 1998. During the course of those years, there were many memorable moments, but two of them stand out particularly in my mind.

The first happened in the late 1980s — probably 1988. Jack and I were in a foursome with Clint Eastwood and his partner, Greg Norman, and we were playing the sixteenth hole at Cypress Point, the famous par 3 that hangs over the Pacific Ocean. Greg Norman and I had hit our balls safely onto the green; Jack and Clint's balls laid up on the left. Clint was on land, but Jack's ball wasn't actually on the turf — it was hung up in what they call an "ice plant," a nasty plant that lurks at the edge of the course.

There must have been two thousand people watching as we rounded the corner and approached our balls. Jack took one look at his lie and said, "I'm going to let it go," a decision of which I approved, since not only was the ball in a plant, the plant was hanging on the edge of a cliff that fell about eighty feet down to the rocks and surf below. Clint Eastwood, however, walked over to the ice plant and took a good hard look. Then, in his best Dirty Harry voice, he said, "Hey, Jack, you can't let that go. You gotta hit that son of a bitch."

Never one to be outdone, Jack grabbed his sand wedge and started to edge his way over the side of the cliff so he could make his shot. I panicked. Here was one of America's greatest actors about to fall to his death, and on my watch. I turned to Clint and said, "We can't let this happen."

"Don't worry," Clint said. Then he calmly walked over and grabbed Jack's belt in the back, hanging on to Jack in a way that allowed him to make a swing. I took a look at this situation and thought, Oh great — now we're going to lose two of America's greatest actors. So I went over and grabbed the back of Clint Eastwood's pants. Then Greg Norman ran over and grabbed the back of my pants, followed by his caddy, Pete Bender, who grabbed the back of Greg's pants. So there was this fivesome, with everybody holding on to each other's pants while Jack Lemmon was swinging away.

Well lo and behold, Jack makes a great swing and connects with the ball, sending it back to the middle of the fairway. The people around us went crazy. Jack high-fived everybody and pumped his fist, and we all laughed, both relieved and amazed.

Back on terra firma, Jack walked over to his ball, which was now resting about forty yards from the green. Once again he took out his sand wedge and made a mighty swing — and shanked the ball right off the cliff and into the ocean, where obviously it was meant to be.

My other story about Jack isn't actually about playing golf, although it did take place on a golf course, this time in Oregon at the Fred Meyer Challenge at the Portland Golf Club. I was playing with Jack in the pro-am portion of the tournament, and we were on the eleventh hole when Jack noticed a porta-potty to the right of the fairway. He waved to me and said, "I'm going to make a pit stop. I'll be right with you."

There were about four or five people waiting to use the toilet, so Jack very politely went to the back of the line. The woman who was standing at the front of the line stopped paying attention to the line and turned to stare at Jack Lemmon, as did everyone else. Jack, ever the gentleman, nodded to the line ahead of him and stood patiently, awaiting his turn.

Then the woman at the head of the line asked if he wouldn't like to go first, considering he was playing golf. Jack accepted the offer and thanked the lady just as someone emerged from the john, allowing him to go in. After the john door had slammed shut, the lady seemed to realize that here was *the* Jack Lemmon and she hadn't had the presence of mind to take his picture. So only seconds after he had gone inside, she yanked the door open and snapped a picture. Since I never saw the photo myself, I don't know what position Jack was in when the lady opened the door, but his hand did appear and calmly shut the door again, this time locking it. We convulsed with laughter, of course, but for Jack Lemmon it was just another day at the golf course. Both the moment and the man were classic.

I loved Jack. He gave me my first complete set of golf clubs. Appropriately enough, they had his name on them, "Jack Lemmon — Unique," and he would occasionally threaten to find out where I'd be playing so he could report his clubs as having been stolen. Eventually I stopped using them, not because I thought he might actually have me arrested; I was afraid I'd lose one, and I couldn't bear that.

If you had spent more than ten minutes with Jack, chances are you would've heard about the AT&T Pro-Am Golf Tournament, and his multidecade effort to make "the cut" — the cut being the number you had to beat on the third day of the event in order to continue to play on the fourth and final day. It's a great achievement for the merely mortal amateurs, and for Jack it was the holy grail.

The first year I played the AT&T, Dan Pohl, my partner and a PGA touring pro, said as we were approaching the eighteenth tee at Pebble Beach, "You know we're gonna make the cut, don't you?" That possibility hadn't even occurred to me because having listened to Jack, I didn't think it was actually possible to make the cut. I was filled with excitement to be so close to achieving something that seemed unattainable, and a moment later, filled with dread that I should accomplish this thing on my first time out. How could I tell Jack?

Walking down the fairway, I realized it'd be easy to tell Jack because he'd be so proud of me. As we made our way up to the green, there he was, backlit by the afternoon sun, his hands on his hips. I waved a warm greeting to him and he replied, "You're gonna make the cut you asshole."

So, it was with a little more relief than remorse that I called him later and told him that we had missed the cut by one stroke. He replied, "Well, there's always next year."

We first met in February 1986, on the first day of rehearsal for a production of *Long Day's Journey Into Night*, which would keep us together for the better part of a year as we performed first on Broadway, then at London's West End, in Tel Aviv, and at a few other stops along the way. We worked together several more times after that in films and on TV.

Any nerves I may have felt on that first day of rehearsal for the O'Neill play were greatly relieved by my own ignorance. Of all Jack's film work, I had only seen *Save the Tiger* and at the time had been a little too young to fully appreciate it. Knowing his list of accomplishments, however, I couldn't help but wonder why at this point in his life, and after having achieved so much, he would choose to play James Tyrone, one of the giants in American dramatic roles, one already immortalized by Fredric March and Laurence Olivier.

It wasn't until midway through our run in Washington, D.C., that I caught up on some of Jack's movies and realized that he is truly one of the giants, and not once had he ever made me feel like I was walking in his shadow — even though I was. He confirmed for me that greatness in our profession doesn't necessarily come at the cost of dignity, humanity, or generosity.

The fourth act of *Long Day's Journey Into Night* has some great speeches, and some highly charged and revealing father-and-son moments. Jack and I loved those scenes, and like most actors, we rarely felt that we had done them justice. I felt closer to him during those scenes than at any other time — even on the golf course. One night, in London, Jack was amazing. The actor disappeared and James Tyrone showed up. I couldn't take my eyes off him. After the curtain came down, he and I lingered onstage. The other actors had left, and he turned to me with tears in his eyes and said, "What did I do?" He paused. "How can I do it again?"

I was so surprised and moved to see this great actor who had already received Oscars, Tonys, Emmys, and many other awards still longing for another chance to get it right, desperate to find that path to one more moment of grace — that magic moment when a performance transports an audience, and takes the actors along for the ride. He reassured me in that moment that it really is all about the work — not the awards, not anything else. And sometimes not even he had all the answers, but he never stopped looking.

Just before the camera would roll, or before a stage entrance, Jack would say, mostly to himself, "Magic time!" These days, when I'm waiting for the camera to roll or for my entrance cue, I can still hear him saying, "Magic time," and I realize that all the time I had been lucky enough to spend with Jack Lemmon was truly that.

About the Author

CHRIS LEMMON is a writer and actor. He lives in Connecticut with his wife and three children. *A Twist of Lemmon* is his first book.

2006

Dear Jack —

We miss you! Jr

Loved your films - Mrs. M.